THE

CENTENARY

OF

AMERICAN METHODISM:

A SKETCH OF ITS HISTORY, THEOLOGY, PRACTICAL SYSTEM, AND SUCCESS.

PREPARED BY ORDER OF THE CENTENARY COMMITTEE OF THE GENERAL CONFERENCE OF THE METHODIST EPISCOPAL CHURCH.

BY ABEL STEVENS, LL.D.

WITH A STATEMENT OF THE PLAN OF THE CENTENARY CELEBRATION OF 1866,

BY JOHN M'CLINTOCK, D.D.

New York:
PUBLISHED BY CARLTON & PORTER,
200 MULBERRY-STREET.
1866.

Entered according to Act of Congress, in the year 1865, by

CARLTON & PORTER,

in the Clerk's Office of the District Court of the United States for the Southern District of New York.

DEDICATORY PREFACE.

OLIVER HOYT, ESQ.

MY DEAR SIR:—Aside from our personal friendship and those distinguished services which have connected your name with some of the most important interests of the Church, I deem it proper to submit this work to you as the author of the resolution, in the Cleveland meeting of the Centenary Committee, appointing me to "prepare a centenary volume, setting forth such facts and showings as should properly come within the scope of such a work;" and the Rev. Dr. M'Clintock, "to co-operate" with me "by adding a chapter embodying the action of the Centenary Committee, and reflecting the spirit which pervaded its discussions."

The Committee were doubtless determined, in their choice of a writer of the proposed book, by the fact that it has been my task foi a number of years to prepare for the denomination a "History of the Religious Movement of the Eighteenth Century, called Methodism," etc., and "The History of the Methodist Episcopal Church in the United States of America." In the familiarity with the historical facts of Methodism which these writings have afforded me, I have found, however, my chief difficulty in preparing the present volume. There is so much that is heroic, and even romantic, in the early history of Methodism, that a writer, in whose mind such data are fresh and vivid, must be perplexed to know where to stop, what to record, or, at least, what to omit. Unless he would risk the design of his work, by its magnitude and consequent high price, he must, with whatever reluctance, omit names sacredly memorable, and incidents as marvelous as any in modern religious history. I have been able to relieve myself from this embarrassment at last only by binding myself rigidly to the practical design of the volume: to the preparation of such a brief yet comprehensive exhibit of Methodism as might most directly promote the purposes of the Centenary Celebration, by showing the true character and claims of the Church, and by setting them forth in such manner that they shall be intelligible to the most uninformed reader. As stated in the Introduction, I have also avoided, as much as possible, except in the last chapter of the volume, any merely didactic treatment of its subjects, but have studied to give it throughout popular attraction and effect, by historical facts and style. The first three chapters, however, are alone in purely narrative or chronological form, and are such only so far as the founding of Methodism in England and America is concerned, or as they can best answer historically the question, What is Methodism? by showing its evangelical stand-point. This chronological narrative could not be further extended without making the work too large; and it must be borne in mind that it is the *founding* of Methodism that is to be celebrated in the Centenary Jubilee. Its subsequent results are classified and embodied in other chapters. It would seem desirable that the good and, in many instances, truly great men who have built up the denomination during its first century, should have some record in the volume, but this is obviously impossible; they have their place in its history, but this is not its history.

I indulge the hope that you, and other readers, who have followed me through my larger works on Methodism, will not find this more compendious and more classified review of its first century in America uninteresting, though it must necessarily be, to a great extent, a repetition of my former data, and in some instances, with but slight modifications of style. The similar books, officially published by different branches of the denomination at its General Centenary in 1839, have been retained as manuals in their literature. I have endeavored to secure to the present volume the same advantage, by so presenting the history and official statistics of the various institutions and interests of the Church as to make the book a permanent standard for reference, affording, in the most convenient form, the chief data which may be needed by writers, preachers, or others, respecting its history, theology, discipline, literature, education, missions, Sunday-schools, etc.

I shall always consider it no small honor to have co-operated, however slightly, with you and your colleagues of the Centenary Committee in the onerous labors with which you have been preparing the Church for its approaching festival, an occasion which I doubt not will be rendered forever memorable.

Respectfully,

ABEL STEVENS.

MAMARONECK PARSONAGE, *Oct.*, 1865.

CONTENTS.

INTRODUCTION .... Page 9

PART I.

WHAT IS METHODISM?—THE QUESTION HISTORICALLY ANSWERED.

CHAPTER I.

ITS ORIGIN, FOUNDERS, AND EARLY PROGRESS IN ENGLAND.

Page
Its Historical Stand-point..... 11
Sketches of John and Charles Wesley..... 11
Susannah Wesley..... 11
Studies and Religious Inquiries of the Wesleys..... 13
John Wesley's Charities..... 20
Sketch of Whitefield..... 21
Conversion of the Wesleys..... 25
Peter Boehler..... 31
Luther on Faith..... 33
Beginning of the Methodist Mission..... 38
Religious Condition of England. 43
Remarkable Scenes..... 48
Lay Preachers..... 51
The first Society..... 52
Persecutions..... 53
Whitefield in America..... 55
Results..... 57

CHAPTER II.

ORIGIN, FOUNDERS, AND PROGRESS IN AMERICA.

The Irish Palatines..... 64
Philip Embury..... 66
Methodism in New York..... 69
Barbara Heck..... 69
Captain Webb..... 70
Outspread of Methodism..... 75
Robert Strawbridge..... 77
Early Local Preachers..... 79

CHAPTER III.

EARLY EVANGELISTS.

Robert Williams..... 83
John King..... 87
Boardman and Pilmoor..... 89
Wright and Asbury..... 90
Asbury's Character..... 91
Rankin and Shadford..... 95
Other Preachers..... 96
The Revolutionary War..... 96

CHAPTER IV.

RAPID PROGRESS.

Methodism in the West..... 102
Episcopal Organization..... 102
Methodism in New England.. 103
In Canada..... 103
Its Native Ministry..... 104
Subsequent Progress..... 105
Remarkable Statistics..... 106
Comparative Strength in different parts of the Country..... 107

CHAPTER V.

ITS PRACTICAL SYSTEM.

"The United Society"..... 109
The "Class Meeting"..... 109
"General Rules"..... 109
Church Officers..... 110
Circuits, Districts, Conferences 111

Page
Vigor of its System........... 113
Its Origin and Development.. 114
Lay Representation........... 120

CHAPTER VI.

ITS DOCTRINAL SYSTEM.

Articles of Religion.......... 125
Arminianism................. 127
Witness of the Spirit......... 128
Christian Perfection.......... 130
Catholicity of Methodism..... 134
Examples of Wesley's Liberality.................... 139
Scientific Theology........... 140
Watson and Warren.......... 140
Relative Position of Methodist Theology.................. 140

PART II.

WHAT HAS METHODISM ACHIEVED ENTITLING IT TO THE PROPOSED COMMEMORATION?

CHAPTER I.

ITS SPECIAL ADAPTATION AND USEFULNESS TO THE COUNTRY.

Great Growth of Population... 147
The Methodist Itinerancy necessary to meet the Moral Wants of the Country...... 148
Its Remarkable Results....... 150
Its Relative Success.......... 152

CHAPTER II.

ITS LABORS IN THE DIFFUSION OF LITERATURE.

Wesley's Literary Services.... 155
Origin of the Methodist Book Concern.................. 157
Its History.................. 157
Its present Magnitude........ 160
Its Usefulness................ 161

CHAPTER III.

ITS EDUCATIONAL LABORS.

First Methodist School....... 163
Wesleyan Educational Efforts. 164
Theological Schools.......... 165
Early Educational Efforts in America.................. 165
Asbury misrepresented....... 166
History of Education in the Church.................... 167
Results—Statistics 170

CHAPTER IV.

ITS SUNDAY-SCHOOL ENTERPRISE.

Early Methodism and Sunday-Schools.................... 171
Wesley adopts the Institution. 172
Asbury introduces it into America................... 173
History of the Methodist Sunday-School Union.......... 175
Its great Success............. 176
Results—Statistics 176

CHAPTER V.

ITS MISSIONARY LABORS.

Early Methodism and Missions 180
Bishop Coke and Missions.... 181
Great Success................ 184
History of Methodist Missionary Society................ 187
Foreign Missions............. 191
German Methodism........... 196
Present Condition of Methodist Missions................... 198
Results—Statistics 198

CHAPTER VI.

ITS LOYALTY AND PATRIOTIC SERVICES.

Wesley and the Revolution... 201
His change of Opinion........ 201
His Letter to British Cabinet Ministers.................. 201
Methodist E. Church first recognizes the New Government 203
Important change of its Article 203
Methodism asserts the National Sovereignty................ 203
Address to Washington....... 205
His Reply.................... 207
The Antislavery Controversy.. 208

	Page
New York East Conference	209
Services in the War	209
President Lincoln's Testimony	210

CHAPTER VII.

SUMMARY VIEW.

Great Numerical Growth	213
Statistics of the M. E. Church	213
Membership and Ministry	213
Educational Institutions	213
Church Property	213
Book Concern	214
Sunday-School Union	214
Missions	214
Methodist Episcopal Church South	214
Aggregate	215
Other Methodist Bodies	215
General Aggregate	216
Bishop Janes on the Actual State of Methodism	217

PART III.

ITS CAPABILITIES AND RESPONSIBILITIES FOR THE FUTURE.

Its Wealth	225
Demands upon it	225
Prospective Population of the Country	226
Area of the Republic	229
Educational Responsibilities	230
Proportion of Juvenile Population	230
Ministerial Education	232
Church Architecture	233
Religious Art	234
Reunion of Methodist Bodies	236
Church Care of its Children	238
Significant Statistics	238
Pastoral Care of Children	239
Spiritual Mission of Methodism	241
The Centenary Memorial	242

CENTENARY

OF

AMERICAN METHODISM.

INTRODUCTION.

THE American Methodists propose to celebrate, in the year 1866, the completion of the first great cycle of their history, its centenary jubilee. From Maine to California, from Canada to the Gulf of Mexico, they will assemble in their churches for religious ceremonies and pecuniary offerings. What entitles Methodism to this solemn, this national commemoration?

In answering this question it is proposed to show:

First, What is Methodism..

Second, What it has achieved that commends it to such general and grateful recognition.

Third, What are its capabilities for the future, and the consequent responsibilities of its people.

It is not designed to discuss these propositions in

the way of dissertation, but, as far as possible, in a historical form such as shall present the general scope of Methodism, as a historical, a doctrinal, and a practical system; so that the inquirer, who may have heretofore given it no studious attention, shall be able to appreciate its real character and claims.

PART I.

WHAT IS METHODISM?

CHAPTER I.

ITS ORIGIN, FOUNDERS, AND EARLY PROGRESS IN ENGLAND.

METHODISM has been described as "a revival Church in its spirit, a missionary Church in its organization;" a resuscitation of the spiritual life and practical aims of primitive Christianity. This is its genuine standpoint, the only one from which its history and its theological and practical systems can be interpreted. It is implied not only in the characteristic features of its progress, doctrines, and economy, but in the individual history of its founders and other principal agents.

John Wesley, its chief apostle and legislator, was born June 14, 1703, in the Epworth Rectory, Lincolnshire, England. Charles Wesley, one of its ablest preachers, and the author of its Psalmody, now its virtual liturgy throughout the world, was born there, December 18, 1708. Susanna Wesley, their mother, who has been called "the real foundress of Methodism," was distinguished by her rare intellect, her piety, and her domestic management. Her system of household education has been the wonder, if not the admiration, of most historical writers on Methodism. It was her custom to retire with each of her children once a week, for religious conversation and prayer. She has recorded that, on these occasions of devout self-recollection, she felt a peculiar solicitude for her most celebrated child. When not yet seven years old he had providentially been saved from a terrible death. The rectory was burned down at night; all its inmates, except John, had escaped, but he was sleeping in a room which the flames rendered inaccessible. The rector and his family knelt on the ground, in the light of their burning home, and committed the soul of the child to God, when suddenly he appeared at the window of his chamber. A peasant, mounting on the shoulders of another, rescued him at the instant that the roof fell in; two minutes of delay would have deprived the history of the world of the name and achievements of its most remarkable modern religious character. "I do intend," said his grateful mother, in one of the recorded meditations of her weekly retirement and prayer with him, "I do intend to be more particularly careful of the soul of this child that thou hast so mercifully provided for, than ever I have been, that I may do my endeavor to instill into his mind the principles of true religion and virtue. Lord, give me grace to do it sincerely and prudently, and bless my attempt with good success."

In advanced life John Wesley recorded the admiration with which he recalled this faithful mother; the skill with which she managed, with little assistance, and in no little poverty, the daily affairs of her family, comprising thirteen children, all of whom, that attained responsible years, became devoted Christians, and "died in the Lord;" her household school, commenced daily with singing and prayer, and conducted solely by herself with academic regularity; her devotion as family priestess to religious duties; her daily evening hour of retired prayer and converse with her children severally; the prudence and zeal with which she conducted in the absence of her husband a sort of Sunday public worship, in the rectory, for the villagers as well as her family.

It was inevitable that such a training should have impressed, for life, the minds of such men as the two Wesleys. They bore from the rectory tendencies which the world could never reverse. John left the home for the Charterhouse School, London, when eleven years old, and entered Oxford University in his seventeenth year. Charles went to the Westminster school when about eight years of age, and in due time joined his brother at Oxford. Their vigilant mother maintained a frequent correspondence with them. "Now," she wrote, "in good earnest, resolve to make religion the business of your life; for, after all, that is the one thing that, strictly speaking, is necessary. All things besides are comparatively little to the purposes of life. I heartily wish you would now enter upon a strict examination of yourself, that you may know whether you have a reasonable hope of salvation by Jesus Christ. If you have, the satisfaction of knowing it will abundantly reward your pains; if you have not, you will find a more reasonable occasion for tears than can be met with in any tragedy." And now the influence of the saintly example and instructions of this extraordinary woman was made manifest, not only in the uprightness of the general moral conduct of her sons, and their success in study and collegiate honors, but in their extraordinary spirit of religious inquiry and devotion. John was the first to reveal this effect; but his conversations with his brother soon awoke a responsive sympathy in the heart of the latter. They perceived that the religious life is the supreme interest of man, that all else should be subordinated to this, and that without it human life must be a failure, the saddest of problems, nay, a mixed farce and tragedy. They perceived further, not in uncharitableness, but deep self-abasement, that the habitual

Christian life of their country, as well as of themselves, was generally, if not universally, incompatible with the standard of spiritual life prescribed by Christianity and exemplified by the original Church. In fine, the very genius of Methodism, as not an ecclesiastical, nor a theological, but a vital and practical system, was foretokened in the moral history of these young and earnest inquirers.

John gave himself to the best religious reading he could command. Three authors became now his habitual companions, next to his Greek Testament. Bishop Taylor's "Holy Living and Dying," Kempis's "Imitation," and Law's "Serious Call" and "Christian Perfection," agreed with those convictions of the thoroughness and sanctity of the Christian life, which had struck into his inmost consciousness; but these three most remarkable writers, perhaps, since the apostolic age, on Spiritual Christianity, failed in an essential point. They delineated accurately a genuine spiritual life, but did not show the requisite means of its attainment. "They preserve a complete silence," says a good authority, "respecting the faith by which the conscience is purged from dead works, and the very thoughts of the heart are made pure, and therefore leave the reader in the hopeless attempt to practice Christian holiness while he is under the power of sin. He is required to love God with all his heart, but he receives no information concerning the manner in which he is to be saved from the condemnation to which he is liable on account of his past sins, and the carnal mind which is enmity against God." In fine, the great Pauline doctrine of "Justification by Faith," which was the most potential truth of primitive Christianity, and by which Luther restored apostolic life to the Church, was generally inert, if not practically ignored, in the English Church of the day. The Wesleys were now, and for some years, feeling after it as in the dark; they were to find it at last, find it by the help of Luther, its great restorer, and with it begin the "Religious movement of the eighteenth century, called Methodism."

The history of their inner life, at this time, is an exceedingly interesting study, and is important as a preliminary and an exponent of their subsequent public life as founders of Methodism. Bishop Taylor's teachings respecting purity of motive, deeply impressed the mind of John Wesley. "Instantly," he says, "I resolved to dedicate *all* my life to God, all my thoughts and words and actions, being thoroughly convinced that there is no medium; that not only a part but the whole must be a sacrifice to God or to myself, that is, in effect, to the devil." This became the characteristic maxim of his whole subsequent life. He could not accept some of Taylor's sentiments, and his dissent led him more definitively to doctrines which were to be vital in the theology of Methodism. The bishop, like most religious teachers of his day, denied that the Christian could usually be sure of his acceptance with God. Wesley replied: "If we dwell in Christ and Christ in us, which he will not do unless we are regenerate, certainly we must be sensible of it. If we can never have any certainty of our being in a state of salvation, good reason it is that every moment should be spent, not in joy, but in fear and trembling; and then, undoubtedly, in this life we are of all men most miserable. God deliver us from such a fearful expectation! Humility is, undoubtedly, necessary to salvation; and if all these things are essential to humility, who can be humble, who can be saved? That we can never be so certain of the pardon of our sins as to be assured they will never rise up against us, I firmly believe. We know that they will infallibly do so, if we apostatize; and I am not satisfied what evidence there can be of our final perseverance, till we have finished our course. But I am persuaded we may know if we are *now* in a state of salvation, since that is expressly promised in the Holy Scriptures to our sincere endeavors, and we are surely able to judge of our own sincerity." Here was not only his later doctrine of the "Witness of the Spirit," but a clear dissent from the Calvinistic tenet of "final perseverance." His proclivity to Arminianism became quite decided about this time. "As I understand faith," he wrote, "to be an assent to any truth upon rational grounds, I do not think it possible, without perjury, to swear I believe anything unless I have reasonable grounds for my persuasion. Now that which contradicts reason cannot be said to stand upon reasonable grounds; and such, undoubtedly, is every proposition which is incompatible with the divine justice or mercy. What, then, shall I say of predestination? If it was inevitably decreed from eternity that a determinate part of mankind should be saved, and none besides, then a vast majority of the world were only born to eternal death, without so much as a possibility of avoiding it. How is this consistent with either the divine justice or mercy? Is it merciful to ordain a creature to everlasting misery? Is it just to punish a man for crimes which he could not but commit? That God should be the author of sin and injustice, which must, I think, be the consequence of maintaining this opinion, is a contradiction to the clearest ideas we have of the divine nature and perfections." His mother confirmed him in these views, and expressed her abhorrence of the Calvinistic theology. God's prescience, she argued, is no more the effective cause of the loss of the wicked than our foreknowledge of the rising of to-morrow's sun is the cause of its rising. She prudently advised, however, abstinence from these speculations as "studies which tended more to confound than to inform the understanding."

He visited his father's parish at Epworth, and in its rural retirement became more than ever infected with the mysticism of Kempis and Law. He was inclined to the recluse life of the Catholic saints; it was, he says, "the decided temper of my soul." He proposed to himself a secluded school in the Yorkshire Dales, but his vigilant mother checked him, predicting that God would open for him a more important career in the world. He made a journey of some miles to converse with "a serious man," of whom he had heard. "Sir," said this man, as the frank and anxious inquirer stood before him, "you wish to serve God and go to heaven, but remember you cannot serve him alone; you must, therefore, *find* companions, or *make* them; the Bible knows nothing of solitary religion." He returned to Oxford and found them; for his brother, led by his influence, had gathered about him a group of devoted students, and the "Holy Club" was already organized. Its members were soon derisively called "Methodists," for the systematic regularity of their lives, and especially of their religious observances. John immediately became their leader by the tacit recognition of his superior capacity and character. They studied together the Greek Scriptures, the classics, and theology; they fasted twice a week, and received the Lord's supper every Sunday. Wesley drew up for them a severe system of self-examination, worthy of a monastic order. They devoted certain hours to the instruction of poor children, the visitation of the sick and prisoners. Wesley himself now began that course of practical charity to the poor which continued to be one of the distinctions of his remarkable life. In a printed sermon he says: "When I was at Oxford, in a cold winter's day, a young maid (one of those we kept at school) called upon me. I said, 'You seem half starved. Have you nothing to cover you but this thin linen gown?' She said, 'Sir, this is all I have.' I put my hand in my pocket, but found I had scarce any money left, having paid away what I had. It immediately struck me, 'Will thy Master say, *Well done, good and faithful steward?* Thou hast adorned thy walls with the money which might have screened this poor creature from the cold! O justice! O mercy! Are not these pictures the blood of this poor maid? See thy expensive apparel in the same light; thy gown, hat, head-dress! Everything about thee which cost more than Christian duty required thee to lay out is the blood of the poor! O be wise for the time to come! Be more merciful! more faithful to God and man! more abundantly adorned with good works!'"

When his income from his college fellowship was

but £30 a year he gave away £2; when it was £60 he still confined his expenses to £28, and gave away £32; when it reached £120 he kept himself to his old allowance, and gave away £92. Besides giving himself wholly to the public good, and laboring as devotedly as any other man of modern times for the moral welfare of the poor, he gave away, it is computed, a hundred and fifty thousand dollars, the proceeds of his publications, etc. The last insertion in his private journal, written with a trembling hand, reads thus: "For upward of eighty-six years I have kept my accounts exactly. I will not attempt it any longer, being satisfied with the continual conviction that I save all I can and give all I can; that is, all I have."

With such rigor did these earnest young men seek self-purification and peace of soul. They were treated with contempt by their fellow-collegians, especially as they marched together to their weekly sacrament; but their number increased, and the germ of the future and world-wide growth of Methodism was already planted within the learned pale of Oxford.

In 1735 a young man joined them, whose fame, as an apostle, was to fill the English realm in both hemispheres. He was born in Gloucester, in 1714, and spent his early life in poverty, ignorance, and vice. When about fifteen years old he became a "common drawer" in an inn at Bristol, (which was kept by his mother,) wearing, as he says, his "blue apron and his snuffers," and "washing and cleaning rooms." "If I trace myself," he adds, "from my cradle to my manhood, I can see nothing in me but a fitness to be damned; and if the Almighty had not prevented me by his grace, I had now either been sitting in darkness, and in the shadow of death, or condemned, as the due reward of my crimes, to be forever lifting up my eyes in torments." Yet he was a youth of the largest soul and the most susceptible moral sensibilities. Religious books fell into his hands; he sought improvement both of heart and head; he made his way to Oxford, where he was now struggling for his education in the humble condition of a servitor, or "poor student." Kempis and Alleine's "Alarm" here deepened his religious solicitude, and, groping in the thick spiritual darkness which surrounded him amid so much intellectual light, he fell into pitiable anguish and not a few superstitious extravagances. His mental struggles seemed at times to impair his faculties; his memory failed; he describes himself as feeling like a person bound in iron armor; he chose the poorest food that he could subsist on, and the meanest raiment, "dirty shoes, patched garments, and coarse gloves," for the mortification of his baffled soul. He almost daily suffered some insult from his fellow-students. When he knelt in prayer he felt a mysterious and insupportable "pressure on soul and body," and often spent hours in these intercessory agonies while the sweat dripped down his person. "God only knows," he says, "how many nights I have lain upon my bed groaning under what I felt. Whole days and weeks have I spent in lying prostrate on the ground, in silent or vocal prayer." For forty days, during Lent, he tasted nothing but coarse bread and sage tea, except on Saturdays and Sundays. He resorted to solitary places seeking rest and finding none; he spent the hours of night praying under the trees, and trembling with cold and mental anguish, till the bell of the college called him to his chamber, where the remaining hours, till dawn, were passed in tears and prayers. Of course his health failed under these errors; a long sickness disabled him to pursue them, and in his helpless prostration he was led to apprehend clearly the doctrine of justification by faith. "God," he says, "was pleased at length to remove the heavy load, to enable me to lay hold on the cross by a living faith, and by giving me the spirit of adoption to seal me, as I humbly hope, even to the day of everlasting redemption. O! with what joy, joy unspeakable, even joy that was full of glory, was my soul filled, when the weight of sin went off, and an abiding sense of the pardoning love of God, and a full assurance of faith, broke in upon my disconsolate soul? Surely it was the day of my espousals, a day to be had in everlasting remembrance. At first my joys were like a spring tide, and, as it were, overflowed the banks; go where I would I could not avoid the singing of psalms almost aloud; afterward they became more settled, and blessed be God, saving a few casual intervals, have abode and increased in my soul ever since."

Such was George Whitefield's initiation into the "Holy Club," the Methodistic band at Oxford. He was to pioneer their public career in England and all along the British colonies of North America, the most eloquent, the most flaming preacher that the Christian Church has known since its apostolic age; a man whose native genius for oratory, heightened by saintly piety, was to shake with an unprecedented sensation, and awaken, as in a moral resurrection, nearly the whole British empire; to extort unwonted admiration, and compliments from Hume, Bolingbroke, Garrick, Walpole, and Chesterfield; to attract in his private ministrations at the mansion of the Countess of Huntington, the nobility of the Court, while it swept like a hurricane over throngs, ten, twenty, forty thousand strong, on the hillsides, and in the market-places of England, Scotland, Wales, Ireland, and North America, startling them to tears, sobs, and irrepressible cries of anguish and penitence. He seems indeed the providential man for the approaching religious crisis. His moral struggles, even the superstitious rigors which came so near destroying him, prepared him to meet and counsel similar cases, in the general religious agitation which was about to set in, to appreciate and assert the true Christian life as "the liberty wherewith Christ hath made us free." With a heart incandescent with divine fire, palpitating with those generous sympathies that render all the world kin and give to the orator irresistible control of the popular mind, he combined an imagination as sublime as that of the Hebraic prophets, and the most extraordinary oratorical aptitudes of voice and gesture. Garrick said he could make his hearers weep or shout with exultation, merely by his varied pronunciation of the word Mesopotamia; Hume said he would go twenty miles to hear him; Chesterfield opened for him his own chapel at Bretby Hall, and theatrical actors resorted to his preaching to study the secret of his unrivaled power. A peasant hearer best characterized perhaps that indescribable power when he declared that Whitefield "preached like a lion."

The Wesleys had a longer preparatory moral struggle. Failing to find rest to their souls in their religious observances and painful self-discipline at Oxford, they resolved to seek it in entire self-sacrifice as missionaries in the ends of the earth. They went in 1735 to Georgia, to preach to the Indians and the colonists of Oglethorpe. On their passage they found that their faith could not sustain them in the perils of storms; though their Moravian fellow-passengers—humble peasants and artisans—sang hymns of hope and joy in the expectation of sudden death. John Wesley conversed with them, and saw clearly that he had not yet attained similar piety. On reaching Georgia he was hospitably received by its little Moravian community; Spangenberg, one of their pastors, put to him a searching question: "Does the Spirit of God bear witness with your spirit that you are a child of God?" Wesley was arrested by the inquiry and knew not how to answer it. "Do you know Jesus Christ?" continued Spangenberg. "I know he is the Saviour of the world," responded Wesley. "True," replied Spangenberg, "but do you know that he has saved *you?*" "I hope he has died to save me," rejoined Wesley. Spangenberg only added, "Do you know yourself?" "I do," answered Wesley, "but I fear," he writes, "they were mere words." He lodged with these devout men, and was much impressed with the singular simplicity and purity of their daily life. He witnessed with admiration their ecclesiastical counsels, the election and ordination of a bishop, and writes that as he sat in their little but dignified synod, he forgot the seventeen centuries which had passed since the days of the apostles, and seemed to be in one of those assemblies where form and state were unknown, but where Paul the tentmaker, and Peter the fisherman, presided with the demonstration of the spirit and of power.

Yet even here, amid the pure light of the primitive faith, which these good men had kindled in the wilderness, "he comprehended it not," but sought peace to his troubled soul in ascetic self-denial and the "merit of works." He read daily prayers at five o'clock in the morning, preached and administered the communion at eleven, and read the evening service at three. He refused all food but bread and water, slept on the ground, taught the children in a school, and went barefooted that he might encourage his poor scholars. He was severe to others as well as to himself; his rigors broke down the patience of the people, and he at last retreated from the field discomfited and in despair. His brother had failed in a similar manner, and had returned to England. John followed him about fifteen months later. As he came in sight of Land's End, England, he wrote in his journal: "I went to America to convert the Indians, but O! who shall convert me? Who, what is he that will deliver me from this evil heart of unbelief? I have a fair summer religion; I can talk well, nay, and believe myself, while no danger is near; but let death look me in the face and my spirit is troubled, nor can I say, to die is gain. I think verily, if the Gospel be true, I am safe; for I not only have given and do give all my goods to feed the poor—I not only give my body to be burned, drowned, or whatever else God shall appoint for me, but I follow after charity—though not as I ought, yet as I can—if haply I may attain it. I now believe the Gospel true. I show my faith by my works, by staking my all upon it. I would do so again and again a thousand times, if the choice were still to make. Whoever sees me, sees I would be a Christian. Therefore are my ways not like other men's ways; therefore I have been, I am, I am content to be, a by-word, a proverb of reproach. But in a storm I think, What if the Gospel be not true? Then thou art of all men most foolish. For what hast thou given thy goods, thy ease, thy friends, thy reputation, thy country, thy life? For what art thou wandering over the face of the earth? a dream? a cunningly-devised fable? O! who will deliver me from this fear of death? What shall I do? Where shall I fly from it? Should I fight against it by thinking, or by not thinking of it? A wise man advised me some time since, 'Be still, and go on.' Perhaps this is the best; to look upon it as my cross; when it comes to let it humble me, and quicken all my good resolutions, especially that of praying without ceasing; and at other times to take no thought about it, but quietly to go on in the work of the Lord." On the 1st of February, 1738, he was again in England, and writing in his diary: "This, then, have I learned in the ends of the earth—that I 'am fallen short of the glory of God;' that my whole heart is 'altogether corrupt and abominable,' and, consequently, my whole life—seeing it cannot be that an 'evil tree' should 'bring forth good fruit;' that, 'alienated' as I am from 'the life of God,' I am a 'child of wrath,' an heir of hell; that my own works, my own sufferings, my own righteousness, are so far from reconciling me to an offended God, so far from making any atonement for the least of those sins which 'are more in number than the hairs of my head,' that the most specious of them need an atonement themselves, or they cannot abide his righteous judgment; that 'having the sentence of death' in my heart, and having nothing in or of myself to plead, I have no hope but that of being justified freely, 'through the redemption that is in Jesus;' I have no hope, but that if I seek, I shall find Christ, and 'be found in him, not having my own righteousness, but that which is through the faith of Christ, the righteousness which is of God by faith.'"

Again he writes, "It is now two years and almost four months since I left my native country, in order to teach the Georgian Indians the nature of Christianity. But what have I learned myself, meantime? Why, what I the least of all suspected, that I, who went to America to convert others, was never myself converted to God. *I am not mad*, though I thus speak, but I *speak the words of truth and soberness*, if, haply, some of those who still dream may awake, and see that as I am so are they." Were they read in philosophy? he continues with eloquent earnestness, and in language which would cover boastfulness itself with shame; were they read in philosophy? so was he. In ancient or modern tongues? he was also. Were they versed in the science of divinity? he too had studied it many years. Could they talk fluently upon spiritual things? the very same could he do. Were they plenteous in alms? behold, he gave all his goods to feed the poor. Did they give of their labor as well as their substance? he had labored more abundantly. Were they willing to suffer for their brethren? he had thrown away his friends, reputation, ease, country; he had put his life in his hands, wandering into strange lands; he had given his body to be devoured by the deep, parched up with heat, consumed by toil and weariness, or whatsoever God should please to bring upon him. But, he continues, does all this, be it more or less it matters not, make him acceptable to God? Does all he ever did, or can, *know*, *say*, *give*, *do*, or *suffer*, justify him in His sight? If the oracles of God are true, if we are still to abide by the *law and testimony*, all these things, though when ennobled by faith in Christ they are holy, and just, and good, yet without it are *dung* and *dross*. He refuses to be comforted by ambiguous hopes. "If," he adds, "it be said that I have faith, for many such things have I heard from many miserable comforters, I answer, so have the devils a *sort* of faith; but still they are strangers to the covenant of promise. The faith I want is a sure trust and confidence in God, that, through the merits of Christ, my sins are forgiven, and I reconciled to the favor of God."

Methodism is indebted to Moravianism for not only some of the most important features of its moral discipline, but for the personal "conversion" of both the Wesleys. On returning to London they found representatives of that community conducting certain social religious assemblies, which met weekly. To these they resorted, especially to one held in Fetter Lane, for they found there a better exposition of Christianity than at St. Paul's or Westminster Abbey, more responsive at least to those religious solicitudes which were quickening their souls into regenerated life. Peter Böhler, afterward a Moravian bishop, became now the daily companion and counselor of the two inquirers. Charles Wesley was the first to emerge, under his guidance, out of the mists which had so long hung about them, into the true light and peace of the Gospel, but not without much hesitancy, and certain theological fallacies which would seem incredible to the better instruction which Methodism has afforded to our age. He was dangerously ill, and Böhler came to sympathize with him. After praying at his bedside, the good Moravian took his hand and asked, "Do you hope to be saved?" "I answered, Yes." "For what reason do you hope to be saved?" "Because I have used my best endeavors to serve God." He shook his head and said no more. I thought him very uncharitable, saying in my heart, What, are not my endeavors a sufficient ground of hope? Would he rob me of my endeavors? I have nothing else to trust to." Some time after this interview, while still uncertain of his life, the great truth of justification by faith dawned clearly upon his vision, he believed, and "entered into rest." "I now," he writes, "found myself at peace with God." His brother still cleaves to Böhler, "not losing an opportunity of conversing with him." They go to Oxford and converse in Latin on divine themes, in the University cloisters and adjacent groves. After one of these walks, Wesley records, "By him, in the hand of the great God, I was on Sunday [March 5th, 1738] clearly convinced of unbelief, of the want of that faith whereby alone we can be saved." Böhler has himself left an account of these interviews, and says that Wesley "wept bitterly while I was talking upon this subject, and afterward asked me to pray with him. I can freely affirm, that he is a poor broken-hearted sinner, hungering after a better righeousness than that which he has hitherto had, even the righteousness of Christ. In the evening he preached from the words, 'We preach Christ crucified,' etc. He had more than four thousand hearers, and spoke in such a way that all were amazed—many souls were awakened."

On the evening of the 24th of May, 1738, Wesley attended one of the social religious assemblies of the Moravians, where he says "one was reading Luther's Preface to the Epistle to the Romans." It was this original protest of the Reformation, in behalf of the doctrine of justification by faith, that led Wesley into the personal experience of that great truth and kindled it on all the altars of Methodism. The venerable document has never been cited by any of the historians of the denomination or biographers of Wesley,* yet it deserves attention not only for its historical connection with the denomination, but for its clear, bold, and genuinely Lutheran statement of the doctrine. "Faith alone," it says, "justifies, and it alone fulfills the law. For faith, through the merits of Christ, obtains the Holy Spirit. This blessed Spirit renews, exhilarates, excites, and inflames the heart, so that it spontaneously performs what the law requires. And then, at length, from the faith thus efficaciously working and living in the heart, freely *fluunt*, proceed those works which are truly good. The apostle

* It is inserted in the Appendix of Jackson's "Centenary of Wesleyan Methodism."

wishes to convey this meaning in the third chapter. For after he had, in that chapter, utterly condemned the works of the law, and might almost seem, by the doctrine of faith, about to destroy and abolish the law, he at once anticipates the objection by asserting, 'We do not destroy the law, but we establish it;' that is, we teach how the law is really fulfilled by believing, or through faith.

"But true faith is the work of God in us, by which we are born again and renewed, through God and the Spirit of God, as we are told in John i; and by which the old Adam is slain, and we are completely transformed *per omnia*, in all things; as the Apostle declares, 'We are made new creatures in Christ through faith;' *ubi*, in which new creatures the Holy Spirit becomes *vita et gubernatio cordis*, the living and ruling principle of the heart. But faith is an energy in the heart; at once so efficacious, lively, breathing, and powerful, as to be incapable of remaining inactive, but bursts forth into operation. Neither does he who has faith, *moratur*, demur about the question, whether good works have been commanded or not; but even though there were no law, feeling the motions of this living impulse putting forth and exerting itself in his heart, he is spontaneously borne onward to work, and at no time does he cease to perform such actions as are truly pious and Christian. But whosoever from such a living affection of the heart produces no good works, he is still in a state of total unbelief, and is a stranger to faith; as are most of those persons who hold long disputes, and give utterance to much declamation in the schools about faith and good works, 'neither understanding what they say, nor whereof they affirm.' Faith, then, is a constant *fiducia*, trust in the mercy of God toward us; a trust living and efficaciously working in the heart; by which we cast ourselves entirely on God, and commit ourselves to him; by which, *certò freti*, having an assured reliance, we feel no hesitation about enduring death a thousand times. And this firm trust in the mercy of God is *tam animosa*, so animating, as to cheer, elevate, and excite the heart, and to transport it with certain most sweet affections toward God, and it animates this heart of the believer in such a manner that, firmly relying on God, he feels no dread in opposing himself *solum*, as a single champion, against all creatures. This high and heroical feeling, therefore, *hos ingentes animos*, this noble enlargement of spirit, is injected and effected in the heart by the Spirit of God, who is imparted [to the believer] through faith. And hence we also obtain [the privilege] to be impelled to that which is good, by this vital energy in our hearts. We also obtain such a cheerful *propensionem*, inclination, that freely and spontaneously we are eager and most ready to do, to suffer, and to endure all things in obedience to a Father and God of such great clemency; who, through Christ, has enriched us with such abundant treasures of grace, and has almost overwhelmed us with such transcendent benefits. It is impossible that this efficacious and vital principle of faith can be in any man without continually operating, and producing fruit to God. It is just as impossible for a pile of dry fagots to be set on fire without emitting flames of light. Wherefore use watchfulness, *ibi*, in this quarter, so as not to believe the vain imaginations of thy own mind, and the foolish cogitations and trifles of the sophists. For these men possess neither heart nor brains: they are mere animals of the belly, born only for these solemn banquets of the schools. But do thou pray to God, who by his word has commanded light to shine out of darkness, that he would be pleased to shine into thy heart, and create faith within thee; otherwise thou wilt never believe, though thou shouldest spend a thousand years in studying to fabricate such cogitations about a faith already obtained or to be hereafter acquired."

Such were the passages of Luther which, we may infer from Wesley's allusions, were read when at "about a quarter before nine, while he was describing the change which God works in the heart through faith in Christ, I felt my heart strangely warmed; I felt I did trust in Christ, Christ alone, for salvation; and an assurance was given me that he had taken away *my* sins, even *mine*, and saved *me* from the law of sin and death. I began to pray with all my might for those who had in a more especial manner despitefully used me, and persecuted me. I then testified openly to all there what I now first felt in my heart."

Böhler had sailed for America; but Wesley's mother, now residing, a widow, in London, was his faithful and most trusted counselor. He read to her a record of his new experience; she emphatically approved it, and exclaimed that "she heartily blessed God, who had brought him to so just a way of thinking." Thus in the thirty-fifth year of his age, after twenty-five years, as he tells us, of religious struggles, he found peace to his soul, by the clearer apprehension of the apostolic doctrine of faith and its relation to justification. And now he was prepared to go forth on his memorable career, publishing through the realm, to all contrite men, the same peace on the same condition. The next month he was preaching "salvation by faith" before the University of Oxford.

I have treated, somewhat in detail, this early portion of the history of Methodism, because it affords us the true standpoint of the new movement. Its origin is to be traced to the Lutheran, not to the Calvinistic conception of Christianity. It was personal spiritual life that its founders sought and obtained, a fact that characterizes all its subsequent development. The formal organization which it afterward assumed tends indeed to disguise this, its essential character; to casual readers of its history, it appears as an ecclesiastical system, as definitive sects, as great hierarchical Churches in Europe and America; but let it be repeated that the reproduction of the apostolic spiritual life was its single aim; and its complicated and singularly powerful organization was but an effect of this its primary fact or principle, an energetic scheme for the propagation of spiritual religion in the Churches and throughout the world.

"What was the rise of Methodism?" asked Wesley, in his conference of 1765. He answered, "In 1729 my brother and I read the Bible; saw inward and outward *holiness* therein; followed after it, and incited others so to do. In 1737 we saw this holiness comes by *faith*. In 1738 we saw we must be *justified* before we are sanctified. But still *holiness* was our point; inward and outward holiness. God then thrust us out to raise a *holy* people."

John Wesley hastened, after his conversion, to the continent, to consult with the Moravians, whose English representatives had thus far been his best guides. He conversed with Count Zinzendorff and other leaders of the United Brethren, and returned to England confirmed in his faith and the now single purpose of his life.

Whitefield had been preaching in Bristol, London, and some country towns, with extraordinary effect;

seldom or never had so great hosts of people assembled in England to hear a preacher; he had stirred the whole metropolis; he had also hastened across the Atlantic and initiated in Georgia his great American mission, which was to quicken all the colonies and prepare the way for the later work of American Methodism. He was now on his way back to England, at the opportune moment to co-operate with the Wesleys. Charles Wesley had also preached in London and elsewhere with much interest during his brother's absence in Germany; his congregations had been crowded, but church after church had been closed against him by the clergy, who could not condemn his doctrines, but rebuked his zeal and disapproved the eager interest and excitement of the people. He was compelled at last to resort to the prisons and the religious "society meetings," which have been mentioned, and which now, more than ever, seemed a providential provision for the incipient Methodism. When John Wesley reached the city he resorted to these humble assemblies as to an asylum. The next day after his arrival "I began," he says, "to declare in my own country the glad tidings of salvation, preaching three times, and afterward expounding to a large company in the Minories. On Monday I rejoiced to meet our little society, which now consisted of thirty-two persons. The next day I went to the condemned felons in Newgate, and offered them a free salvation. In the evening I went to a society in Bear Yard, and preached repentance and remission of sins. The next evening I spoke the truth in love at a society in Aldersgate-street; some contradicted at first, but not long; so that nothing but love appeared at our parting. Thursday, 21st, I went to a society in Gutter Lane, but I could not declare the mighty works of God there as I did afterward at the Savoy, with all simplicity, and the word did not return empty. On Saturday, 23d, I was enabled to speak strong words both at Newgate and at Mr. E.'s society, and the next day at St. Anne's, and twice at St. John's, Clerkenwell, so that I fear they will bear with me there no longer." Thus he entered upon the great career of his life; for these incessant labors, it has been justly observed, were no consequence of a febrile or temporary zeal; they were an example of what was thereafter to be almost his daily habit till he fell, in his eighty-eighth year, at the head of more than a hundred and fifty thousand followers, and five hundred and fifty itinerant preachers, who were stimulated by his unabated zeal to similar labors in both hemispheres. He began by "expounding," nearly every day, in the London "Societies." On Sundays he preached in the churches, but, at the end of almost every sermon, he records it to be the last time; not that his manner was clamorous, or in any way eccentric; nor that his doctrine was heretical, for it was clearly that of the Homilies and other standards of the Church; but it was brought out too forcibly and presented too vividly for the state of religious life around him. He went from the closed pulpits not only to the "Societies," but to the prisons and the hospitals, where his message was received with gratitude and tears, and was attended with the demonstration of the Spirit and of power.

Denied the city pulpits, the brothers went not only to the "Societies" and prisons, but to and fro in the country, preaching almost daily. Whitefield was needed to lead them into more thorough and more necessary "irregularities." He arrived in London December 8, 1738. Wesley hastened to greet him, and on the 12th "God gave us," he writes, "once more to take sweet counsel together." The mighty preacher who had agitated the whole metropolis a year before, now met the same treatment as his Oxford friends. In three days five churches were denied him. Good, however, was to come out of this evil. He also had recourse now to the "Societies," and his ardent soul caught new zeal from their simple devotions as from his new trials. Wesley describes a scene at one of these assemblies, which reminds us of the preparatory Pentecostal baptism of fire, by which the apostles were "endued with power from on high" for their mission. He says, January

1, 1739, that Messrs. Hall, Kinchin, Ingham, Whitefield, and his brother Charles were present with him at a love-feast in Fetter Lane, with about sixty of their brethren. "About three in the morning, as they were continuing instant in prayer, the power of God came mightily upon them, insomuch that many cried out for exceeding joy, and many fell to the ground. As soon as they had recovered a little from the awe and amazement which the presence of the Divine Majesty had inspired, they broke out with one voice, "We praise thee, O God; we acknowledge thee to be the Lord." Whitefield exclaims: "It was a Pentecostal season, indeed." And he adds, respecting these "Society meetings," that "sometimes whole nights were spent in prayer. Often have we been filled as with new wine, and often have I seen them overwhelmed with the Divine Presence, and cry out, 'Will God indeed dwell with men upon earth? How dreadful is this place! This is no other than the house of God, and the gate of heaven!'" In this manner did the three evangelists begin together the memorable year which was afterward to be recognized as the epoch of Methodism. On the 5th Whitefield records an occasion which foreshadowed the future. A "conference" was held at Islington with seven ministers, "despised Methodists," concerning many things of importance. They continued in fasting and prayer till three o'clock, and then parted "*with a full conviction that God was about to do great things among us.*"

Was it necessary that these predicted "great things" should be done in England at this time? The moral condition of the United Kingdom in the last century is well known. Citations from indisputable authorities, to prove its general demoralization, have become trite passages in works on Methodism. The reaction against Puritanism, produced by the restoration of the Stuarts, had left a universal moral blight upon the nation. Seldom or never had gross vice been more rife among the masses of the people, seldom or never had the Churches and their clergy sunk into more complete moral stupor, not to say moral death. Bishop Burnet declares that he was "oppressed night and day" with "sad thoughts" on the prospects of Christianity in the realm. "I cannot," he adds, "look on without the deepest concern, when I see the imminent ruin hanging over this Church, and, by consequence, over the whole Reformation. The outward state of things is black enough, God knows; but that which heightens my fears rises chiefly from the inward state into which we are unhappily fallen." Referring to the character of the clergy, he says, "Our ember weeks are the burden and grief of my life. The much greater part of those who come to be ordained are ignorant to a degree not to be apprehended by those who are not obliged to know it. The easiest part of knowledge is that to which they are the greatest strangers. Those who have read some few books, yet never seem to have read the Scriptures. Many cannot give a tolerable account even of the Catechism itself, how short and plain soever. This does often tear my heart. The case is not much better in many who, having got into orders, come for institution, and cannot make it appear that they have read the Scriptures, or any one good book, since they were ordained." Watts declares that there was "a general decay of vital religion in the hearts and lives of men;" that "this declension of piety and virtue" was common among Dissenters and Churchmen; that it was "a general matter of mournful observation among all who lay the cause of God to heart;" and he called upon "every one to use all possible efforts for *the recovery of dying religion in the world.*" Another writer asserts that "the Spirit of God has so far departed from the nation, that hereby almost all vital religion is lost out of the world." Another says, "The religion of nature makes up the darling topics of our age; and the religion of Jesus is valued only for the sake of that, and only so far as it carries on the light of nature, and is a bare improvement of that kind of light. All that is restrictively Christian, or that is peculiar to Christ, (everything concerning him that has not its apparent foundation in natural light, or that goes beyond its principles,) is waived, and banished, and despised." Archbishop Secker says: "In this we cannot be mistaken, that an open and professed disregard is become, through a variety of unhappy causes, the distinguishing character of the present age." "Such," he declares, "are the dissoluteness and contempt of principle in the higher part of the world, and the profligacy, intemperance, and fearlessness of committing crimes, in the lower, as must, if this torrent of impiety stop not, become absolutely fatal." He further asserts that "Christianity is ridiculed and railed at with very little reserve, and the teachers of it without any at all;" and this testimony was made but one year before that which is commemorated as the epoch of Methodism. About the same time Butler published his great work on the Analogy between Religion and the Constitution and Course of Nature, as a check to the infidelity of the age. In his preface he gives a deplorable description of the religious world. He concurs with the preceding authorities in representing it as in the very extremity of decline. "It has come," he says, "to be taken for granted that Christianity is no longer a subject of inquiry; but that it is now at length discovered to be fictitious. And accordingly it is treated as if, in the present age, this were an agreed point among all persons of discernment, and nothing remained but to set it up as a principal subject for mirth and ridicule." Southey says: "The clergy had lost that authority which may always command at least the appearance of respect; and they had lost that respect also by which the place of authority may sometimes so much more worthily be supplied. In the great majority of the clergy zeal was wanting. The excellent Leighton spoke of the Church as a fair carcass without a spirit. Burnet observes that, in his time, our clergy had less authority, and were under more contempt, than those of any other Church in all Europe; for they were much the most remiss in their labors, and the least severe in their lives. It was not that their lives were scandalous; he entirely acquitted them of any such imputation; but they were not exemplary, as it became them to be; and in the sincerity of a pious and reflecting mind, he pronounced that they would never regain the influence they had lost till they lived better and labored more."

A scarcely less prejudiced writer on Methodism, Isaac Taylor, admits that when Wesley appeared the Anglican Church was "an ecclesiastical system under which the people of England had lapsed into heathenism, or a state hardly to be distinguished from it;" and that Methodism "preserved from extinction and reanimated the languishing Nonconformity of the last century, which, just at the time of the

Methodistic revival, was rapidly in course to be found nowhere but in books."

This general decline had reached its extremity when Wesley and his coadjutors appeared. "It was," to use his own words, "just at the time when we wanted little of filling up the measure of our iniquities, that two or three clergymen of the Church of England began vehemently to call sinners to repentance." "What," he asks, "is the present characteristic of the English nation? It is ungodliness. Ungodliness is our universal, our constant, our peculiar character."

There was, in fact, a profound infidelity undermining British Christianity at this time; it was the chief cause of the inefficiency of the pulpit, of the declension of the Churches, and of the popular demoralization. Moreover, it really gave birth to the later skepticism of Germany and of Europe generally. The writings of Hobbes, Shaftesbury, Tindal, and Collins, were in prevalent circulation, and were reinforced by the three mightiest giants, in skeptical error, which modern times have produced, Bolingbroke, Hume, and Gibbon. Natural religion was the favorite study of the clergy, and of the learned generally, and included most of their theology. Collins and Tindal had denounced Christianity as priestcraft; Whiston pronounced the miracles to be Jewish impositions; Woolston declared them to be allegories; and the next year after the recognized date of Methodism, Edelmann and Reimarus introduced the English deism into Germany, and thus founded the Rationalism which, as developed by her "Historical" or "Negative Criticism," nearly extinguished, for a time, her religious life. The decayed state of the English Church, in which Methodism was about to have its birth, was, in fine, the cause, direct or indirect, of most of the infidelity of the age, both at home and abroad. Arianism and Socinianism, taught by such men as Clarke, Priestley, Price, and Whiston, had become fashionable among the best English thinkers. Many illustrious names can be cited as exceptions; they were, however, but exceptions to the general condition of religion throughout the United Kingdom. Some of the most emphatic testimonies, to the deplorable declension of piety and morals, which have come down to us, are from the pens of such exceptional men.

The Methodistic movement may be said to have now definitively commenced. Whitefield went to Bristol; the whole city seemed aroused by his powerful preaching, but he was soon repelled from its pulpits. He betook himself to its jails, alms-houses, and public grounds, where the common people "heard him gladly." He went to the neighboring Kingswood Mines, and there began that reformation and evangelization of the colliers of England, which has been one of the greatest honors of Methodism. The miners came forth unwashed from their caverns and crowded about him to hear his open-air sermons, weeping till their tears traced "white gutters" down their cheeks. All the surrounding country felt the sensation of his wonderful eloquence, and his congregations "on the mounts" comprised thousands and tens of thousands; "the hedges and trees were full." His sonorous voice rung to their utmost limit; they stood "in an awful manner around the mount," hushed into profound silence, and he was reminded by the spectacle of "the scene of the general assembly" of the last day. He sent to London for Wesley, who, on arriving, scrupled as a rigid churchman about "out-door preaching." But he soon saw that it was a providential necessity. What else could he and his associates do? The churches were closed against them, and the people were perishing in ignorance and vice. He followed Whitefield's example, and having once preached in the open air, he had crossed the Rubicon, never to retreat. Field preaching, with all its consequences, was now to be the first great practical measure of Methodism, and with it the whole realm was to be stirred.

Whitefield, leaving Wesley among the blackened colliers of Kingswood, hastened into Wales, where Howell Harris, a young man who had been driven from Oxford University by its infidelity and its scoffings at his religious earnestness, was going to and fro preaching in its villages, though he was not in Holy Orders. His example seemed a strange, a providential coincidence with the new movement at London, Bristol, and Kingswood. Whitefield seized his hand and bade him "God speed." They traversed the principality together, preaching in churches, in the grave-yards, in the market-places, on the mountain sides. Other evangelists co-operated with them, chiefly Griffith Jones, and Daniel Rowlands "the Welsh thunderer." Wales, which had been as demoralized as any other part of the United Kingdom, was thoroughly aroused by these itinerants, and rose as in a moral resurrection under the subsequent labors of Methodism. The new denomination, distinguished into two sections, as Calvinistic and Arminian, now predominates in the country. Wales had at the beginning of the century but twenty-three dissenting Churches; they have multiplied to twenty-five hundred; more than twelve hundred of them are Methodistic. A chapel dots every three square miles of its territory, and over a million of people, nearly the whole population, attend public worship some part of every Sunday. Wales has been religiously renovated by the Methodistic movement.

Whitefield returned to London, where he and Wesley took the open field at Moorfields and

Kennington Common. Their congregations were estimated at twenty, forty, sometimes fifty thousand. The singing of the vast multitudes could be heard two miles off, Whitefield's voice a mile. The lowest masses of the neglected people were thus invaded by the Gospel; hundreds and thousands were reclaimed to virtue and piety and incorporated in the London "Societies." It was not long before the evangelists were abroad in all England, Scotland, Wales, and Ireland, surprising and arousing the Churches, and the population generally, by their unwonted measures and zeal, and thus was inaugurated the greatest "religious revival" of modern ages.

Lay preachers were rapidly raised up from among the converts of the movement: Thomas Maxfield, Thomas Richards, Thomas Westell, John Nelson, and others, the pioneers of that army of thousands and tens of thousands of lay itinerants whose proclamation of the truth has since resounded through much of both hemispheres, and is daily sounding further and further toward the ends of the earth. Like their great leaders, they traveled over the realm preaching by day and by night. Their artless but earnest ministry secured the attention of the common people, and it was apparent that they wielded a power which belonged not to the established pulpit. Wesley as their superintendent and guide was almost ubiquitous in the land, preaching twice or thrice daily, beginning at five o'clock in the morning. "Societies" were formed in order to bring their numerous converts into relations of Christian communion and discipline. Being excluded from the churches, they were compelled to meet in the open air till they began the erection of chapels. On May 12, 1739, the foundations of the first Methodist chapel in the world were laid, with prayers and songs of praise, at Bristol; in November of the same year, the "Foundry," in London, was consecrated. The former was begun first, though the latter was opened first. Wesley had no thought yet of a sect or a schism; he was a stanch churchman; he opened these edifices as temporary accommodations of his converts, and only because the clergy of the establishment compelled him to do so, by excluding him and his associates from its pulpits and sacramental altars. The chapel in Bristol bore the humble name of "The Preaching House," that in London its former title of the "Old Foundry."

The year in which these chapels were opened is considered to be the epoch of Methodism. In his "Church History," Wesley assigns it other dates, as the formation of "the Holy Club," at Oxford, in 1729; and the meeting of himself and others, by the advice of Peter Böhler, in Fetter Lane, May 1, 1738; but in his introduction to the "General Rules of the Society," he says, "In the latter end of the year

1739, eight or ten persons came to me in London and desired that I would spend some time with them in prayer, and advise them how to flee from the wrath to come; this was the rise of the UNITED SOCIETY." "This," he tells us, "was soon after the consecration of the Foundry." Twelve came the first night, forty the next, and soon after a hundred. Though he continued in fraternal relations with the Moravian "Societies" at London, till July 20, 1740, the society, formed the preceding year, was organized and controlled by himself, and has continued in unbroken succession down to our day. The date of its origin was celebrated with centenary solemnities by all the Methodist communities of the world in 1839. It was signalized not only by the organization of the Society, by the opening of the Foundry for worship, and by the erection at Bristol of the first Methodist chapel, but by the organization of "Bands" in that city, and the publication, by the Wesleys, of their "Hymns and Sacred Poems," the beginning of that Methodistic psalmody which has since been of inestimable service to the denomination, wherever it has extended, as its virtual liturgy.

It was not long before "societies," and chapels or "preaching houses," as they were unpretentiously called, began to rise more or less in all parts of the country. Hostilities also arose; mobs assailed the itinerants; their chapels were pulled down: for months, and even for years, riots were of almost constant occurrence. In some sections the rabble moved in hosts from village to village, attacking preachers and people, destroying not only the churches, but the homes of Methodists. In Staffordshire "the whole region was in a state little short of civil war." In Darlaston, Charles Wesley could distinguish the houses of the Methodists by their marks of violence as he rode through the town. At Walsall he saw the flag of the rioters waving in the market-place, their headquarters. In Lichfield "all the rabble of the country was gathered together, and laid waste all before them." The storm swept over nearly all Cornwall. Newcastle was in tumult. In London even occurred formidable mobs. In Cork and Dublin they prevailed almost beyond the control of the magistrates. Methodism had, in fine, to fight its way over nearly every field it entered in Great Britain and Ireland. The clergy and the magistrates were often the instigators of these tumults. Not a few of the itinerants were imprisoned, or impressed into the army and the navy; some were martyred. But the devoted sufferers held on their way till they conquered the mob, and led it by thousands to their humble altars. Howell Harris, amid storms of persecution, succeeded, as we have seen, in planting Methodism in Wales, where it has elevated the popular religious condition, once exceedingly low, above that of Scotland. Wesley traversed Ireland as well as Great Britain. He crossed the channel forty-two times, making twenty-one visits; and Methodism has yielded there some of its best fruits. Whitefield, known as a Calvinist, and forming no societies, was received in Scotland. His congregations were immense, filling valleys or covering hills, and his influence quickened into life its Churches. He continued to aid Harris in founding Calvinistic Methodism in Wales. The whole evangelical dissent of England still feels his power. With the Countess of Huntingdon, he founded the Calvinistic Methodism of Great Britain; but such was the moral unity of both parties, the Arminian and the Calvinistic, that the essential unity of the general Methodistic movement was maintained, awakening to a great extent the spiritual life of both the national Church and of the Nonconformists, and producing most of those "Christian enterprises" by which British piety has since been spreading its influence around the globe. The British Bible Society, most of the British Missionary Societies, Tract Societies, the Sunday-school, religious periodicals, cheap popular literature, negro emancipation, Exeter Hall with its public benefits and follies, all arose directly or indirectly from the impulse of Methodism.

Whitefield crossed the Atlantic thirteen times and

journeyed incessantly through the colonies, passing and repassing from Georgia to Maine like a "flame of fire." The Congregational Churches of New England, the Presbyterians and the Baptists of the Middle States, and the mixed colonies of the South, owe their later religious life and energy mostly to the impulse given by his powerful ministrations. The "great awakening" under Edwards had not only subsided before Whitefield's arrival, but had reacted. Whitefield restored it; and the New England Churches received under his labors an inspiration of zeal and energy which has never died out. He extended the revival from the Congregational Churches of the Eastern to the Presbyterian Churches of the Middle States. In Pennsylvania and New Jersey, where Frelinghuysen, Blair, Rowland, and the two Tennents had been laboring with evangelical zeal, he was received as a prophet from God, and it was then that the Presbyterian Church took that attitude of evangelical power and aggression which has ever since characterized it. These faithful men had begun a humble ministerial school in a log-cabin "twenty feet long and nearly as many broad." "The work is of God," said Whitefield, "and therefore cannot come to naught." The fame of Princeton has verified his prediction. "Nassau Hall received a Methodistic baptism at its birth; Whitefield inspirited its founders, and was honored by it with the title of A.M.; the Methodists in England gave it funds; and one of its noblest presidents (Davies) was a correspondent of Wesley, and honored him as a 'restorer of the true faith.'" Dartmouth College arose from the same impulse. It received its chief early funds from the British Methodists, and bears the name of one of their chief Calvinistic associates, whom Cowper celebrated as "The one who wore a coronet and prayed." Whitefield's preaching, and especially the reading of his printed sermons in Virginia, led to the founding of the Presbyterian Church in that state, whence it has extended to the South and South-west. "The stock from which the Baptists of Virginia and those in all the South and South-west have sprung was also Whitefieldian." The founder of the Freewill Baptists of the United States was converted under the last preaching of Whitefield.

Such are but glimpses of the progress of British Methodism before its organization in America. It became apparent that a new epoch had occurred in the history of English Christianity. Under the influence of Whitefield and the Countess of Huntingdon the Calvinistic nonconformity of the realm arose as from the dead to new life, which has continued ever since with increasing energy; by the same means, with the co-operation of Wesley, a powerful evangelical party was raised up in the Establishment, and most of the measures of evangelical propagandism which have since kept British Christianity alive with energy, and have extended its activity to the foreign world, are distinctly traceable to this great "revival." Meanwhile its reformatory power among the English common people had become unquestionable and marvelous to all candid observers. It has been remarked that at about the end of its first decade a scarcely paralleled religious interest had been spread and sustained throughout the United Kingdom and along the Atlantic coast of America. Not only had the Churches of both countries been extensively reawakened, but the great fact of a Lay Ministry had been accomplished—great not only in its direct results, but perhaps more so by its reacting shock, in various respects, against the ecclesiasticism which for fifteen hundred years had fettered Christianity with bands of iron. It had presented before the world the greatest pulpit orator of the age, if not of any age—Whitefield; also one of the greatest religious legislators of history—Wesley; a hymnist whose supremacy has been but doubtfully disputed by a single rival—Charles Wesley; and the most signal example of female agency in religious affairs which Christian history records—the Countess of Huntingdon. The lowest abysses of the English population among colliers and miners had been reached by the Gospel. Calvinistic Methodism was restoring the decayed nonconformity of England.

Wesleyan Methodism, though adhering to the Establishment, had taken an organic and permanent form; it had its Annual Conferences, Quarterly Conferences, Class Meetings and Band Meetings; its Watch-nights and Love-feasts; its Traveling Preachers, Local Preachers, Exhorters, Leaders, Trustees, and Stewards. It had districted England, Wales, and Ireland into Circuits for systematic ministerial labors, and now commanded a ministerial force of about seventy men. It had fought its way through incredible persecutions and riots, and had won at last a general, though not universal peace. Its Chapels and Preachers' houses, or parsonages, were multiplying over the country. It had a rich Psalmody, which has since spread wherever the English tongue is used; and a well-defined Theology, distinguished by two notable features that could not fail to secure popular interest, namely, that it transcended the prevalent creeds in both *spirituality* and *liberality;* in its experimental doctrines of Conversion, Sanctification, and the Witness of the Spirit, and in the evangelical liberalism of its Arminianism. It had begun its present scheme of Popular Religious Literature, had provided the first of that series of Academic institutions which has since extended with its progress, and was contemplating a plan of Ministerial Education, which has been effectively accomplished. Already the despondent declarations of Watts, Secker, and Butler, respecting the prospects of religion, might be pronounced no longer relevant. Yet Watts had been dead but two years, and Secker and Butler still survived.

At the end of the third decade, the year in which it sent its first missionaries to America, it enrolled more than twenty-eight thousand members and one hundred and twelve lay traveling preachers, besides the Wesleys and their clerical coadjutors.

Wesley lived to see his cause established in the United States with an episcopal organization, planted in the British North American Provinces, and in the West Indies, and died at last, in 1791, with his system apparently completed, universally effective and prosperous, sustained by five hundred and fifty itinerant and thousands of local preachers, and more than a hundred and forty thousand members, and so energetic that many men, who had been his co-laborers, lived to see it the predominant body of Dissenters in the United Kingdom and the British Colonies, the most numerous Church of the United States of America, and successfully planted on most of the outlines of the missionary world.

In 1839 was celebrated the hundredth anniversary of English Methodism. The English Methodists appointed the 25th of October as a day of festive religious observance throughout their Churches in all parts of the world. Pecuniary contributions for certain great interests of the Church were called for, and the call was answered by a liberality never before equaled in any one instance in their history, if, indeed, in the history of any other Christian body. The Wesleyans gave one million and eighty thousand dollars. The American Methodists gave six hundred thousand. On the appointed day Methodists throughout the earth met in their temples to thank God for his blessings upon the first cycle of their history. Signal indeed had been those blessings. Wesley, as we have seen, died in 1791, at the head of a host of 550 itinerant preachers, and 140,000 communicants in the United Kingdom, the British Provinces, in the United States, and the West Indies; at the centenary, less than half a century later, the denomination had grown to more than 1,171,000, including about 5,200 itinerant preachers, in the Wesleyan and Methodist Episcopal Churches; and, comprising the various bodies bearing the name of Methodists, to an army of more than 1,400,000, of whom 6,080 were itinerant preachers. Its missionaries, accredited members of Conferences, were about three hundred and fifty, with nearly an equal number of salaried, and about three thousand unpaid assistants. They occupied about three hundred stations, each station being the head of a circuit. They were laboring in Sweden, Germany, France, Cadiz, Gibraltar, Malta, Western and Southern Africa, Ceylon, continental India, New South Wales, Van Dieman's Land, New

Zealand, Tonga, Habai Islands, Vavou Islands, Fiji Islands, the West Indies. They had under instruction in their mission schools about fifty thousand pupils, and in their mission Churches were more than seventy thousand communicants. At least two hundred thousand persons heard the Gospel regularly in their mission chapels. The Methodist missionaries were now more numerous than the whole Wesleyan ministry as enrolled on the Minutes of Wesley's last Conference, and their missionary communicants were about equal to the whole number of Methodists in Europe at that day. Wesley presided over Methodism during its first half century and two years more; during the remainder of the century it reproduced, in its missions alone, the whole numerical force of its first half century. Thus far it had demonstrated its providential mission as a revival of apostolic spiritual life and apostolic propagandism.

CHAPTER II.

ORIGIN, FOUNDERS, AND PROGRESS OF METHODISM IN AMERICA.

THOUGH Wesley sent no missionaries to America till 1769, the true epoch of American Methodism dates three years earlier.

The humbleness of its origin, contrasted with the greatness of its results, presents perhaps as striking an example as ecclesiastical history affords since the apostolic age, of the scriptural truth, that "God hath chosen the weak things of the world to confound the things which are mighty, and low things of the world, and things which are despised, hath God chosen, yea, and things which are not, to bring to naught things that are: that no flesh should glory in his presence." The History of the Methodist Episcopal Church records that, in 1758, John Wesley visited the county of Limerick, Ireland; that his Journal reports there a singular community, settled in Court Mattress, and in Killiheen, Balligarrane, and Pallas, villages within four miles of Court Mattress; that they were not native Celts, but a Teutonic population, and that having been nearly half a century without pastors who could speak their language, they had become thoroughly demoralized: noted for drunkenness, profanity, and "utter neglect of religion." But the Methodist itinerants had penetrated to their hamlets, and they were now a reformed, a devout people. They had erected a large chapel in the center of Court Mattress. "So did God at last provide," writes Wesley, "for these poor strangers who, for fifty years, had none who cared for their souls." At later visits he declares that three such towns as Court Mattress, Killiheen, and Balligarrane were hardly to be found anywhere else in Ireland or England. There was "no cursing or swearing, no Sabbath breaking, no drunkenness, no ale-house in any of them." "They had become a serious, thinking people, and their diligence had turned all their land into a garden. How will these poor foreigners," he adds, "rise up in the day of judgment against those that are round about them!" But the most interesting fact respecting this obscure colony was not yet apprehended by Wesley, or he would have wondered still more at their providential history. The Methodism of the New World was already germinating among them; in about two years the prolific seed was to be transplanted to the distant continent, and at the time of Wesley's death (about thirty years later) its vigorous boughs were to extend over the land from Canada to Georgia, from the Atlantic to the Mississippi, sheltering more than sixty-three thousand Church members, and two hundred and fifty itinerant preachers. In about thirty years after Wesley's death (1820) American Methodism was to advance to the front of the great "movement" with a majority of more than seventeen thousand over the parent Church, including all its foreign dependencies, and thenceforward the chief numerical triumphs of the denomination were to be in the western hemisphere.

The "Palatines," as these German-Irishmen are usually called, were driven from the Palatinate, on the Rhine, by the Papal troops of Louis XIV. They found refuge within the lines of Marlborough, and were provided for by Queen Anne, some in England, some in Ireland, some in America. The Teutonic Methodists in the county of Limerick, who were destined to found American Methodism, were descendants of the persecuted Protestants whom the Papal zeal of the Grand Monarch had expatriated; his attempt to suppress Protestantism in the Palatinate led thus to one of the most energetic developments of Protestantism in the modern history of religion. "On a spring morning in 1760," says an Irish writer, "a group of emigrants might have been seen at the custom-house quay, Limerick, preparing to embark for America. At that time emigration was not so common an occurrence as it is now, and the excitement connected with their departure was intense.

They were Palatines from Balligarrane, and were accompanied to the vessel's side by crowds of their companions and friends, some of whom had come sixteen miles to say 'farewell' for the last time. One of those about to leave—a young man, with a thoughtful look and resolute bearing—is evidently the leader of the party, and more than an ordinary pang is felt by many as they bid him farewell. He had been one of the first-fruits of his countrymen to Christ, had been the leader of the infant Church, and in their humble chapel had often ministered to them the word of life. He is surrounded by his spiritual children and friends, who are anxious to have some parting words of counsel and instruction. He enters the vessel, and from its side once more breaks among them the bread of life. And now the last prayer is offered; they embrace each other; the vessel begins to move. As she recedes uplifted hands and uplifted hearts attest what all felt. But none of all that vast multitude felt more, probably, than that young man. His name is Philip Embury. His party consisted of his wife, Mary Switzer, to whom he had been married on the 27th of November, 1758, in Rathkeale Church; two of his brothers and their families; Peter Switzer, probably a brother of his wife; Paul Heck, and Barbara his wife; Valer Tettler; Philip Morgan, and a family of the Dulmages. The vessel arrived safely in New York on the 10th of August,

1760. Who that pictures before his mind that company of Christian emigrants leaving the Irish shore but must be struck with the simple beauty of the scene? Yet who among the crowd that saw them leave could have thought that two of the little band were destined, in the mysterious providence of God, to influence for good countless myriads, and that their names should live long as the sun and moon endure? Yet so it was. That vessel contained Philip Embury, the first class-leader and local preacher of Methodism on the American continent, and Barbara Heck, 'a mother in Israel,' one of its first members, the germ from which, in the good providence of God, has sprung the Methodist Episcopal Church of the United States; a Church which has now more or less under its influence about seven millions of the germinant mind of that new and teeming hemisphere! 'There shall be a handful of corn in the earth upon the top of the mountains; the fruit thereof shall shake like Lebanon: and they of the city shall flourish like grass of the earth.'"

In 1752 Philip Embury heard John Wesley preach in Ireland; and of the same year, a manuscript fragment, in his own hand-writing, says, "On Christmas Day, being Monday, the 25th December, in the year 1752, the Lord shone into my soul, by a glimpse of his redeeming love, being an earnest of my redemption in Christ Jesus, to whom be glory for ever and ever.

Amen!" He was respected for his probity and obliging manners; he studied the elements of knowledge under both English and German teachers, and afterward learned the craft of a carpenter, in which, it is said, he became skillful. Soon after his conversion he was licensed as a local preacher, and ministered to his countrymen in their Irish settlements. He was modest and shrunk from responsibility. On arriving at New York it is probable, though not certain, that he endeavored to keep up the religious communion of his Methodist fellow-immigrants; but the temptations of their new condition prevailed against him; they fell away, and he seems to have become discouraged, and not to have used his office as a "local preacher" till the autumn of 1766. Dr. Roberts, who has made this part of our history a special study, says, "the families who accompanied him were not all Wesleyans—only a few of them; the remainder were members of the Protestant Church in Ireland, but made no profession of an experimental knowledge of God, in the pardon of sin and adoption. After their arrival in New York, with the exception of Embury and three or four others, they all finally lost their sense of the fear of God, and became open worldlings. Some subsequently fell into greater depths of sin than others. Late in the year 1765 another vessel arrived in New York, bringing over Paul Ruckle, Luke Rose, Jacob Heck, Peter Barkman, and Henry Williams, with their families. These were Palatines, some of them relatives of Embury, and others his former friends and neighbors. A few of them only were Wesleyans. Mrs. Barbara Heck, who had been residing in New York since 1760, visited them frequently. One of the company, Paul Ruckle, was her eldest brother. It was when visiting them on one of these occasions that she found some of the party engaged in a game of cards; there is no proof, either direct or indirect, that any of them were Wesleyans, and connected with Embury. Her spirit was roused, and, doubtless emboldened by her long and intimate acquaintance with them in Ireland, she seized the cards, threw them into the fire, and then most solemnly warned them of their danger and duty. Leaving them, she went immediately to the dwelling of Embury, who was her cousin. It was located upon Barrack-street, now Park Place. After narrating what she had seen and done, under the influence of the Divine Spirit and with power she appealed to him to be no longer silent, but to preach the word forthwith. She parried his excuses, and urged him to commence at once in his own house, and to his own people. He consented, and she went out and collected four persons, who, with herself, constituted his audience. After singing and prayer he preached to them, and enrolled them in a class. He continued thereafter to meet them weekly. Embury was not among the card-players, nor in the same house with them."

Embury's house could not accommodate all the hearers who soon flocked to it; he hired therefore a larger room in the neighborhood, providing for the rent by gratuitous contributions, and preaching without compensation. In a short time he had organized "two classes," of six or seven members each. He extended his labors, preaching in other places, particularly the almshouse, where the poor heard him gladly.

In the early part of the next year the humble pastor and his congregation were surprised by the appearance among them of a British officer in his regimentals; his reverent demeanor soon assured them that he had come not to interfere with, but to share their worship. At its close he introduced himself as Captain Thomas Webb, "of the King's service, but also a soldier of the Cross, and a spiritual son of John Wesley." They were overjoyed, and hailed him as a "brother beloved." The good captain had fought at Louisburg and at Quebec; at the latter he had been wounded in the arm, and at the former had lost his right eye, over which he now wore a shade. After these perils he returned to England and heard Wesley preach in Bristol; he became a regenerated man, and was licensed by Wesley as a local preacher. During the remainder of his life he was one of the most active evangelists of Methodism, preaching in England, Ireland, and America till his death in 1796. Asbury called him "an Israelite indeed." "He is a man of fire," wrote Wesley, "and the power of God constantly accompanies his word." He heard Webb in the Old Foundry, London, and writes, "I admire the wisdom of God in still raising up various preachers, according to the various tastes of men. The captain is all life and fire; therefore although he is not deep or regular, yet many, who would not hear a better preacher, flock to hear him, and many are convinced under his preaching." He records, again, that he had "kindled a flame" in Bath, "and it has not yet gone out." "I found his preaching in the street in Winchester had been blessed greatly. Many were more or less convinced of sin, and several had found peace with God. I never saw the house before so crowded with serious and attentive hearers." For eleven or twelve years we catch glimpses of the military evangelist in the Journals of Wesley. The last of them is in 1785, when, being at Salisbury, where the captain had recently preached, he "endeavored to avail himself of the fire which" that veteran "seldom failed to kindle." Fletcher of Madeley appreciated him, and tried hard with him to induce Benson, the commentator, to throw himself into the Methodistic movement in America.

Fletcher himself, doubtless by the influence of Webb, had strong thoughts of doing so, but his health forbade it. The allusions to Webb in the cotemporary publications of Methodism show that he was a man of profound piety. "He experienced much of the power of religion in his own soul," says an itinerant who usually lodged at his home in England; "he wrestled day and night with God for that degree of grace which he stood in need of that he might stand firm as the beaten anvil to the stroke, and he was favored with those communications from above which made him bold to declare the whole counsel of God. His evidence of the favor of God was so bright that he never lost a sense of that blessed truth, 'the blood of Jesus Christ cleanseth us from all sin.' For him to live was Christ, to die was gain." John Adams, the statesman of the American Revolution and President of the Republic, heard him with admiration, and describes him as "the old soldier, one of the most eloquent men I ever heard; he reaches the imagination and touches the passions very well, and expresses himself with great propriety." By another hearer he is spoken of as "a perfect Whitefield in declamation." A high Methodist authority, who knew the captain well, says, "They saw the warrior in his face, and heard the missionary in his voice. Under his holy eloquence they trembled, they wept, and fell down under his mighty word." One of

Wesley's veterans, who was intimate with the captain, and who read the funeral service over his coffin, says, " Great multitudes crowded to hear him, and a vast number in different places owned him for their spiritual father. His ministry was plain, but remarkably powerful; he was truly a Boanerges, and often made the stout-hearted tremble."

Such was the stranger in uniform, whose sudden appearance startled the little assembly of Embury's hearers. He had heard of them at Albany, where he had lived a short time before as barrack-master, and where he had opened his house for religious services, conducted by himself. He had hastened to New York to encourage the struggling society. Following the custom of the times, he always wore his military dress in public. He preached in it, with his sword lying on the table or desk before him. The populace were attracted by the spectacle, and soon crowded the preaching-room beyond its capacity. A rigging loft, sixty feet by eighteen, on William-street, was rented in 1767. Here Webb and Embury preached thrice a week to crowded assemblies. "It could not contain half the people who desired to hear the word of the Lord."

A chapel was necessary. Barbara Heck, the real foundress of American Methodism, and who, from the day that she recalled Embury to his duty, had guarded the incipient cause with the vigilance of a priestess, was the first to suggest such a provision; Webb seconded her proposal. She even submitted a plan of the humble edifice, one which she believed God approved and had suggested to her while praying on the subject. "I the Lord will do it," was the response to her supplication, which seemed to come to her by inspiration. A site on John-street, ever since sacred, was leased in 1768, and purchased two years later. Subscriptions were made extensively through the city for the expense of the modest edifice. Embury was first on the list of its trustees; he had the honor of being first preacher, first class-leader, first treasurer, and first trustee of the first society of Methodism in the Western hemisphere. The chapel was of stone, faced with blue plaster, sixty feet by forty-two. Embury seems to have been its chief architect; and he labored upon it by the side of the humblest mechanic. On the 30th of October, 1768, he ascended its pulpit, made by his own hands, and dedicated the building with a sermon on Hosea x, 12, "Sow to yourselves in righteousness, reap in mercy, break up your fallow ground, for it is time to seek the Lord, till he come and reign righteousness upon you." The population of the city was about twenty thousand, not too large for a general recognition of the fact that Methodism had now its monumental edifice, however humble, in the midst of them, and John-street chapel has ever since been, not only a sacred memorial of the denomination, but has become one of the most venerable monuments of the city. It was immediately thronged with hearers, and Embury and Webb were its diligent preachers. In about half a year after its dedication an American correspondent of Wesley wrote, "the Lord carries on a very great work by those two men."

Webb made frequent excursions to other parts of the country, and soon became the principal founder of American Methodism. He spent some time preaching at Jamaica, Long Island, where at least "twenty-four persons received justifying grace." He passed often through New Jersey and formed Societies in its chief towns. He was the first Methodist who preached in Philadelphia, where, in 1767 or 1768, he formed a "class" of seven members, in a sail loft, which, as in New York and later in Baltimore, was for some time the only temple of the infant cause. His zeal and liberality led to the purchase, in 1770, of St. George's Church, the first Methodist chapel of the city. In 1769 he founded Methodism in Delaware, preaching in Newcastle, Wilmington, and the forests of the Brandywine. He extended his labors to Baltimore; he corresponded with Wesley, entreating him to send out missionaries to the new field; after some were sent he went to England to obtain a reinforcement, and brought back with him, in 1773, Rankin and Shadford. He plead for America in the British Conference and in the Methodist chapels generally. Down to the outbreak of the Revolution he was, in fine, an apostle to the New World, devoting his whole time here for about nine years to Christian labors. After his final return to England he continued to preach with his early fervor and power till December 20th, 1796, when he suddenly died at Bristol, where he sleeps beneath the pulpit of Portland Chapel, an edifice which was erected chiefly through his own exertions. A monument on its walls commemorates him as "brave—active—courageous—faithful—zealous—successful."

Embury continued to serve the John-street society gratuitously till the arrival of Wesley's first missionaries, in 1769, when he gladly surrendered to them its pulpit. He soon after emigrated with a party of his fellow-Methodists to the town of Salem, Washington county, New York. It is recorded that he there continued to labor as a local preacher, and formed a society, chiefly of his own countrymen, at Ashgrove, the first Methodist class within the bounds of the Troy Conference which in our day reports more than twenty-five thousand communicants, and more than two hundred traveling preachers. He was held in high estimation by his neighbors, and officiated among them not only as a preacher, but as a magistrate.* While mowing in his field in 1775, he injured himself so severely as to die suddenly, aged but forty-five years, "greatly beloved and much lamented," says Asbury. He was buried on the neighboring farm of his Palatine friend, Peter Switzer. After reposing fifty-seven years in his solitary grave without a memorial, his remains were disinterred with solemn ceremonies, and borne by a large procession to the Ashgrove burial ground, where their resting-place is marked by a monument, recording that he "was the first to set in motion a train of measures which resulted in the founding of John-street Church, the cradle of American Methodism, and the introduction of a system which has beautified the earth with salvation, and increased the joys of heaven." Some of his family emigrated to Upper Canada, and, with the family of Barbara Heck, were among the founders of Methodism in that province.

About the time that Embury and Webb were laying the foundations of the denomination in New York, Robert Strawbridge was inaugurating it in Maryland. Like Embury, he also was an Irishman, and was characterized by the native ardor of his countrymen. He was eloquent, and a melodious

* "In a map (now before me) of the Province of New York, copied from a London map dated 1779, that locality is laid off as a manor, bearing the name of Embury."—*Rev. P. P. Harrower to the Author.*

singer; he loved adventure and travel, and as an evangelist went to and fro preaching night and day. He arrived in this country at some time between 1760 and 1765, and settled on "Sam's Creek," in Frederick county, Maryland, which had but recently been reclaimed from the perils of savage invasion. He opened his house for preaching; formed in it a Methodist society; and, not long after, built the "Log Meeting-house" on Sam's Creek, about a mile from his home. He buried beneath its pulpit two of his children. It was a rude structure, twenty-two feet square, and, though long occupied, was never finished, but remained without windows, door, or floor. "The logs were sawed on one side for a door-way, and holes were made on the other three sides for windows." He became virtually an itinerant, journeying about in not only his own large county, (then comprehending three later counties,) but in Eastern Maryland, Delaware, Pennsylvania, and Virginia; preaching with an ardor and a fluency which surprised his hearers, and drew them in multitudes to his rustic assemblies. He seemed disposed literally to let the morrow, if not indeed the day, take care of itself. His frequent calls to preach in distant parts of the country required so much of his time that his family were likely to suffer in his absence, so that it became a question with him "Who will keep the wolf from my own door while

I am abroad seeking after the lost sheep?" His neighbors, appreciating his generous zeal and self-sacrifice, agreed to take care of his little farm, gratuitously, in his absence. The Sam's Creek Society, consisting at first of but twelve or fifteen persons, was a fountain of good influence to the county and the state. It early gave four or five preachers to the itinerancy. Strawbridge founded Methodism in Baltimore and Harford counties. The first Society in the former was formed by him at the house of Daniel Evans, near the city, and the first chapel of the county was erected by it. The first native Methodist preacher of the continent, Richard Owen, was one of his converts in this county; a man who labored faithfully and successfully as a local preacher for some years, and who entered the itinerancy at last, and died in it. He was long the most effective co-laborer of Strawbridge, traveling the country in all directions, founding societies, and opening the way for the coming itinerants. Owen's temperament was congenial with that of Strawbridge. He clung to the hearty Irishman with tenacious affection, emulated his missionary activity, and at last followed him to the grave, preaching his funeral service to a "vast concourse," under a large walnut tree.

Several preachers were rapidly raised up by Strawbridge in his travels in Baltimore and Harford counties: Sater Stephenson, Nathan Perigo, Richard Webster, and others; and many laymen, whose families have been identified with the whole subsequent progress of Methodism in their respective localities, if not the nation generally. We have frequent intimations of his labors and success in the early biographies of Methodism, but they are too vague to admit of any consecutive narration of his useful career. We discover him now penetrating into Pennsylvania, and then arousing the population of the Eastern Shore of Maryland; now bearing the standard into Baltimore, and then, with Owen, planting it successfully in Georgetown, on the Potomac, and in other places in Fairfax county, Virginia; and by the time that the regular itinerancy comes effectively into operation in Maryland, a band of preachers, headed by such men as Watters, Gatch, Bowham, Haggerty, Durbin, Garrettson, seem to have been prepared, directly or indirectly, through his instrumentality, for the more methodical prosecution of the great cause. We find his own name in the Minutes in 1773 and 1775 as an itinerant. We trace him at last to the upper part of Long Green, Baltimore county, where an opulent and generous public citizen, Captain Charles Ridgely, who admired his character and sympathized with his poverty, gave him a farm, free of rent, for life. It was while residing here, "under the shadow of Hampton," his benefactor's mansion, that, in "one of his visiting rounds to his spiritual children, he was taken sick at the house of Joseph Wheeler, and died in great peace;" probably in the summer of 1781. Owen, as has been remarked, preached his funeral sermon in the open air, to a great throng, "under a tree at the north-west corner of the house." Among the concourse were a number of his old Christian neighbors, worshipers in the "Log Chapel," to whom he had been a Pastor in the wilderness; they bore him to the tomb, singing as they marched one of those rapturous lyrics with which Charles Wesley taught the primitive Methodists to triumph over the grave. He sleeps in an orchard of the friend at whose house he died—one of his own converts—under a tree, from the foot of which can be seen the great city which claims him as its Methodistic apostle, and which, ever since his day, has been pre-eminent among American communities for its Methodistic strength and zeal.

CHAPTER III.

EARLY EVANGELISTS AND MISSIONARIES.

THE news of the success of Embury, Webb, and Strawbridge reached England and excited no little interest. Wesley was pondering the expediency of sending out missionaries to enter the opening doors; but meanwhile some zealous evangelists, impatient of delay, hastened as volunteers to the new field. The first of them was Robert Williams, a local preacher, who went on board the packet for America, with his saddle-bags, a bottle of milk, and a loaf of bread, but no money for the expense of the voyage. A Methodist fellow-passenger paid the latter. On arriving in New York (1769) Williams immediately began his mission in Embury's Chapel, and thenceforward, for about six years, was one of the most effective pioneers of American Methodism: "the first Methodist minister in America that published a book, the first that married, the first that located, and the first that died." We have but little knowledge of his career, but sufficient to prove that he had the fire and heroism of the original itinerancy. He was stationed at John-street Church some time in 1771. He labored successfully with Strawbridge in founding the new cause in Baltimore county. In the first published Conference Minutes he is appointed to Petersburgh, Va. "He was the apostle of Methodism in Virginia." He followed Strawbridge in founding it in 1772 on the Eastern Shore of Maryland. In the same year he appeared in Norfolk, Va. Taking his stand on the steps of the Court-house, he collected a congregation by singing a hymn, and then preached with a plainness and energy, so novel among them, that they supposed he was insane. No one invited him home, in a community noted for hospitality; they were afraid of his supposed lunacy; but on hearing him a second time their opinion was changed. He was received to their houses, and soon after a society was formed in the city, the germ of the denomination in the state. In 1773 he traveled in various parts of Virginia. Jarrett, an apostolic churchman, and afterward a notable friend of the Methodists, encouraged his labors, and entertained him a week at his parsonage. Williams formed the first circuit of Virginia. A signal example of his usefulness (incalculable in its results) was the conversion of Jesse Lee. He was "the spiritual father" of this heroic itinerant, the founder of Methodism in New England. "Mr. Lee's parents opened their doors for him to preach. They were converted. Two of their sons became Methodist ministers, and their other children shared largely in the blessings of the Gospel, which he proclaimed with such flaming zeal, holy ardor, and great success." The religious interest excited by Williams's labors soon extended into North Carolina, and opened the way for the southward advancement of Methodism. He bore back to Philadelphia, says Asbury, a "flaming account of the work in Virginia: many of the people were ripe for the Gospel and ready to receive us." He returned, taking with him a young man named William Watters, who was thus ushered into the ministry, and has ever since been honored as the first native American itinerant.* Leaving him in the field already opened, Williams went himself southwestward, "as Providence opened the way." Subsequently he bore the cross into North Carolina. He formed a six weeks' circuit from Petersburgh southward, over the Roanoke River, some distance into that state, and thus became the "apostle of Methodism" in North Carolina, as well as Virginia. Like most of the itinerants of that day, he located after his marriage, and settled between Norfolk and Suffolk, where, and in all the surrounding regions, he continued to preach till his death, which occurred on the 26th of September, 1775. Asbury was now in the country, and at hand to bury the zealous pioneer. He preached his funeral sermon, and records in his

* Owen was the first native Methodist preacher, but he did not join the conference or regular itinerancy till after Watters had been received.

Journal the highest possible eulogy on him. "He has been a very useful, laborious man. The Lord gave many seals to his ministry. Perhaps no one in America has been an instrument of awakening so many souls as God has awakened by him." "He was a plain, pointed preacher, indefatigable in his labors," says a historian of the Church. "That pious servant of the Lord," says Watters, his young fellow-traveler in the South. "The name of Robert Williams," says our earliest annalist, "still lives in the minds of many of his spiritual children. He proved the goodness of his doctrine by his tears in public and by his life in private. He spared no pains in order to do good—standing on a stump, block, or log, he sung, prayed, and preached to hundreds" as they passed along from their public resorts or churches. "It was common with him after preaching to ask most of the people, whom he spoke to, some question about the welfare of their souls, and to encourage them to serve God." He printed and circulated Wesley's Sermons, "spreading them through the country, to the great advantage of religion: they opened the way in many places for our preachers, where these had never been before. Though dead, he yet speaketh by his faithful preaching and holy walk." Such was the evangelist who was the first practically to respond to the appeals from America to England. His grave is unknown, but he will live in the history of the Church forever, associated with Embury, Webb, and Strawbridge. He did for it, in Virginia and North Carolina, what Embury did for it in New York, Webb in New Jersey, Pennsylvania, and Delaware, and Strawbridge in Maryland.

Not long after Williams's arrival, John King also came from England. He opened his mission in the Potter's Field of Philadelphia. He extended his labors into Delaware, and soon was co-operating with Strawbridge and Williams, in Maryland. He was the first Methodist who preached in the city of Baltimore. His first pulpit there was a blacksmith's block at the intersection of Front and French streets. His next sermon was from a table at the junction of Baltimore and Calvert streets. His courage was tested on this occasion, for it was the militia training-day, and the drunken crowd charged upon him so effectually as to upset the table and lay him prostrate on the earth. He knew, however, that the noblest preachers of Methodism had suffered like trials in England, and he maintained his ground courageously. The commander of the troops, an Englishman, recognized him as a fellow-countryman, and, defending him, restored order, and allowed him to proceed. Victorious over the mob, he made so favorable an impression as to be invited to preach in the English Church of St. Paul's, but improved that opportunity with such fervor as to receive no repetition of the courtesy. Methodism had now, however, effectively entered Baltimore, down to our day its chief citadel in the new world. In five years after King stood there on the blacksmith's block, it was strong enough to entertain the Annual Conference of the denomination. King was afterward received into the regular itinerancy. He was a member of the first Conference of 1773, and was appointed to New Jersey. He soon after entered Virginia, and with two other preachers traveled Robert Williams's new six weeks' circuit, extending from Petersburgh into North Carolina. "They were blessed among the people, and a most remarkable revival of religion prevailed in most of the circuit," says the cotemporary historian of the Church; "Christians were united and devoted to God; sinners were greatly alarmed: the preachers had large congregations; indeed, the Lord wrought wonders among us that year." Still later we trace him again to New Jersey; he located during the Revolution, but in 1801 reappeared in the itinerant ranks in Virginia. He located finally in 1803. One of our historical authorities assures us that "he was a truly pious, zealous, and useful man, and so continued till his death, which occurred a few years since, at a very advanced age, in the vicinity of Raleigh, N. C. He was probably the only survivor, at the time of his decease, of all the preachers of ante-revolutionary date." John King did valiant service in our early struggles. He seems, however, to have been often led away by his excessive ardor; he used his stentorian voice to its utmost capacity; and it is said that when he preached in St. Paul's, Baltimore, he "made the dust fly from the old velvet cushion." Wesley, who probably knew him in England, and corresponded with him in America, calls him "stubborn and headstrong."

Webb's correspondence with Wesley at last procured the appointment of regular itinerant preachers to America. On the 3d of August, 1769, Wesley announced in the Conference at Leeds, "We have a pressing call from our brethren of New York (who have built a preaching house) to come over and help them. Who is willing to go?" Richard Boardman and Joseph Pilmoor responded, and were sent. They arrived at Philadelphia in October, 1769.

Boardman had been in Wesley's itinerancy about six years, and was now about thirty-one years old. Wesley describes him as "pious, sensible, greatly beloved." Asbury says, he was "kind, loving, worthy, truly amiable, and entertaining, of child-like temper." An old writer on Methodism says, he was "a man of great piety, of amiable disposition, and great understanding." His companion, Pilmoor, was converted in his early youth, was educated at Wesley's Kingswood school, and had now itinerated about four years. He was a man of deep piety, of good insight, and much courage, of a dignified presence and ready discourse.

Whitefield saluted them gladly in America and bade them Godspeed. He had prepared the way for them by awakening a religious interest throughout the colonies. He had made his thirteenth passage of the Atlantic, and the next year after their arrival he died at Newburyport, Mass. He had finished his extraordinary career, and left the field white for the harvest. The Methodist itinerants were now to reap it. Boardman and Pilmoor continued to labor in the country about four years, from Boston to Savannah.

In 1770 "America" is recorded for the first time in Wesley's printed "Minutes of Conference," with four preachers, Boardman, Pilmoor, Williams, and King. In the following year it is recorded with three hundred and sixteen Church members. In the conference of 1771 Wesley again called for volunteers for the new field. "Our brethren in America," he said, "call aloud for help; who will go?" Five responded, and two were sent: Francis Asbury (afterward bishop) and Richard Wright. Of the latter we know but little. He had traveled but one year in the ministry before he came to America; he labored, with more or less success, from New York to Norfolk for three or four years, and then returned to England. But Francis Asbury was destined to be the most historical, the representative character of American Methodism. He was now a young man about twenty-six years of age. He had been in the traveling ministry only about five years, and but four years on the catalogue of regular appointments, but had seen hard service on Bedfordshire, Colchester, and Wiltshire circuits. He was studious, somewhat introspective, with a thoughtfulness which was tinged at times with melancholy. His was one of those minds which can find rest only in labor; designed for great work, and therefore endowed with a restless instinct for it. He was an incessant preacher, of singular practical directness; was ever in motion, on foot or on horseback, over his long circuits; a rigorous disciplinarian, disposed to do everything by method; a man of few words, and those always to the point; of quick and accurate insight into character; of a sobriety, not to say severity, of temperament, which might have been repulsive had it not been softened by a profound religious humility, for his soul, ever aspiring to the highest virtue, was ever complaining within itself over its shortcomings. His mind had eminently a military cast. He never lost his self-possession, and could therefore seldom be surprised. He seemed not to know fear, and never yielded to discouragement in a course sanctioned by his faith or conscience. He could plan sagaciously, seldom pausing to consider theories of wisdom or policy, but as seldom failing in practical prudence. The rigor which his disciplinary predilections imposed upon others was so exemplified by himself, that his associates or subordinates, instead of revolting from it, accepted it as a challenge of heroic emulation. Discerning men could not come into his presence without perceiving that his soul was essentially heroic, and that nothing committed to his agency could fail, if it depended upon conscientiousness, prudence, courage, labor, and persistence. "Who," says one who knew him intimately, "who of us could be in his company without feeling impressed with a reverential awe and profound respect? It was almost impossible to approach him without feeling the strong influence of his spirit and presence. There was something in this remarkable fact almost inexplicable and indescribable. Was it owing to the strength and elevation of his spirit, the sublime conceptions of his mind, the dignity and majesty of his soul, or the sacred profession with which he was clothed, as an embassador of God, invested with divine authority? But so it was; it appeared as though the very atmosphere in which he moved gave unusual sensations of diffidence and humble restraint to the boldest confidence of man." Withal, his appearance was in his favor. In his most familiar portrait he has the war-worn aspect of a military veteran; but in earlier life his frame was robust, his countenance full, fresh, and expressive of generous, if not refined, feelings. He was attentive to his apparel, and always maintained an easy dignity of manners, which commanded the respect, if not the affection, of his associates. The appeals from the American Methodists had reached him in his rural circuits, for he had never left his ministerial work to attend the Annual Conference. Two months before the session of 1771 his mind had been impressed with the thought that America was his destined field of labor. He saw in the new world a befitting sphere for his apostolic aspirations. The great qualities, manifested in his subsequent career were inherent in the man, and Wesley could not fail to perceive them. He not only accepted him for America, but, notwithstanding his youth, appointed him, at the ensuing conference, at the head of the American ministerial itinerancy.

His labors in the New World were, if possible, greater than those of Wesley in the old; he traveled more miles a year and preached as often. On becoming bishop of the Church, he seemed to become ubiquitous throughout the republic. The history of Christianity, since the apostolic age, affords not a more perfect example of ministerial and episcopal devotion than was presented in this great man's life. He preached almost daily for more than half a century. During most of this time he traveled over the continent, with hardly an intermission, from north to south and east to west, directing the growing hosts of his denomination with the skill and authority of a great captain. He was ordained bishop of the Methodist Episcopal Church when thirty-nine years old, at its organization in 1784, when it comprised less than fifteen thousand members and but about eighty preachers; and he fell in 1816, in his seventy-first year, at the head of an army of more than two hundred and eleven thousand members, and more than seven hundred itinerant preachers. It has been estimated that in the forty-five years of his American ministry he preached about sixteen thousand five hundred sermons, or at least one a day, and traveled about two hundred and seventy thousand miles, or six thousand a year; that he presided in no less than two hundred and twenty-four annual conferences, and ordained more than four thousand preachers. He was, in fine, one of those men of anomalous greatness, in estimating whom the historian is compelled to use terms which would be irrelevant, as hyperbole, to most men with which he has to deal. His discrimination of character was marvelous; his administrative talents would have placed him, in civil government or in war, by the side of Richelieu or Cesar, and his success placed him unquestionably at the head of the leading characters of American ecclesiastical history. No one man has done more for Christianity in the western hemisphere. His attitude in the pulpit was solemn and dignified, if not graceful; his voice was sonorous and commanding, and his discourses were often attended with bursts of eloquence "which spoke a soul full of God, and, like a mountain torrent, swept all before it." Notwithstanding his advanced age and shattered health he continued his travels to the last, till he had to be aided up the pulpit steps, and to sit while preaching. On the 24th of March, 1816, when unable to either walk or stand, he preached his last sermon at Richmond, Va., and on the 31st died at Spottsylvania, Va. With Wesley, Whitefield, and Coke, he ranks as one of the four greatest representative men of the Methodistic movement. In American Methodism he ranks immeasurably above all his cotemporaries and successors, in historical importance, and his eventful life affords the chief materials for the history of the Methodist Episcopal Church during half a century.

At Wesley's conference for 1772 Captain Webb made an eloquent appeal for recruits for the ministry in America, and obtained Thomas Rankin and George Shadford. The former was a thorough "disciplinarian," a man of "iron will," and did good service in the colonial societies, by his general enforcement of discipline. Shadford was a preacher of extraordinary unction, the "revivalist" of the times. Each of them traveled and labored indefatigably from New York to North Carolina, till the breaking out of the Revolutionary war, when they returned to England.

Meanwhile other English missionaries arrived: James Dempster, Martin Rodda, and William Glendenning; but the alarm of the approaching revolution dispersed the foreign laborers. Most of them returned to their native country, and there resumed their evangelical travels. A native ministry, however, had now providentially been raised up, consisting of gigantic men, true apostles, peculiarly fitted for the further work of the evangelization of the continent. Watters, Hatch, Abbott, Mann, Lee, Garrettson, Dickins, Dromgoole, and others had either entered the itinerant ranks or were about to do so, and during the storm of the war, while Asbury alone of their foreign coadjutors remained, and he much of the time in concealment, they bore the standard of the cross forward, sometimes into the very camps of the army. The cradle of Methodism was in fact incessantly rocked by the revolutionary storm, and it was the only form of religion that advanced in America during that dark period. In the year (1760) in which Embury and his fellow-

Palatines arrived, the Lords of Trade advised the taxing of the colonies, and the agitations of the latter commenced. The next year James Otis, the "morning star" of the Revolution, began his appeals in Boston for the rights of the people. The following year the whole continent was shaken by the royal interference with the colonial judiciary, especially at New York; and Otis attacked, in the Massachusetts legislature, the English design of taxation as planned by Charles Townshend. Offense followed offense from the British ministry, and surge followed surge in the agitations of the colonies. The year preceding that in which the John-street Church was formed is memorable as the date of the Stamp Act; the Church was founded amid the storm of excitement which compelled the repeal of the act in 1766—the recognized epoch of American Methodism. The next year a new act of taxation was passed which stirred the colonies from Maine to Georgia, and "The Farmer's Letters," by John Dickinson of Pennsylvania, appeared—"the foundation rock of American politics and American statesmanship." In two years more the Massachusetts legislature "planned resistance." Samuel Adams approved of making the "appeal to heaven," of war, and British ships and troops were ordered to Boston. The first Annual Conference of American Methodism was held in the stormy year (1773) in which the British ministry procured the act respecting tea, which was followed by such resistance that the ships bringing that luxury were not allowed to land their cargoes in Philadelphia and New York; were only allowed to store them, not to sell them, in South Carolina, and were boarded in Boston harbor and the freight thrown into the sea. In the next year the Boston Port Bill inflamed all the colonies; "a General Congress" was held; Boston was blockaded; Massachusetts was in a "general rising;" then came the year of Lexington, and Concord, and Bunker Hill, introducing the "War of Revolution," with its years of conflict and suffering. Thus Methodism began its history in America in the storm of the Revolution; its English missionaries were arriving or departing amid the ever increasing political agitation; it was cradled in the hurricane, and hardened into vigorous youth, by the severities of the times, till it stood forth, the next year after the definitive treaty of peace, the organized "Methodist Episcopal Church in the United States of America." Its almost continual growth in such apparently adverse circumstances is one of the miracles of religious history. In 1776 it was equal, in both the number of its preachers and congregations, to the Lutherans, the German Reformed, the Reformed Dutch, the Associate Church, the Moravians, or the Roman Catholics. At the close of the war it ranked fourth or fifth among the dozen recognized Christian denominations of the country. During the war it had more than quadrupled both its ministry and its members. It was a special providential provision for the religious wants of America, and was therefore initiated and trained in the trying circumstances which gave birth and training to the new nation.

CHAPTER IV.

RAPID PROGRESS OF METHODISM IN AMERICA.

METHODISM broke out almost simultaneously, as we have seen, in both the north and middle of the the opening continent. By the end of the Revolutionary war it had laid securely its foundations in both regions. From these its first humble positions it was now rapidly to advance till it should dot the whole country with its temples, and growing with the growth of the population, become the predominant religious faith of the nation. Its history henceforth develops too rapidly and largely to admit of more than a few further allusions in this part of our volume; nor are its details indeed required by the plan of this brief work; for its Churches are about to commemorate its origin in America, and thus far its origin has been sketched.* In other sections of the volume we shall have occasion to present much of its remaining history in outlines of its Disciplinary and

* For its fuller history I must take the liberty of referring the reader to "The History of the Religious Movement, etc., called Methodism,' 3 vols., and "The History of the Methodist Episcopal Church," etc., 2 vols., works in which I have endeavored to gather most of the remains of its annals, and from which I have condensed much of the present volume.

Doctrinal systems. A few additional chronological and statistical statements must here suffice.

In 1773 was held its first Annual Conference, in the city of Philadelphia, consisting of 10 preachers, and reporting 1,160 members of society. In 1781 it crossed the Alleghanies and began that grand work of western evangelization, which has become the most important portion of its subsequent history, giving birth to the "old Western Conference," which extended from the Northern Lakes to Natchez, and every one of whose original "districts" comprehends in our day several conferences. There are now, west of the Alleghanies, 33 conferences, 2,816 traveling preachers, (besides superannuates,) and nearly 438,000 members, not including the Southern and other branches of Methodism.*

In 1784 its first General Conference was held in Baltimore for the organization of "the Methodist Episcopal Church in the United States of America," Dr. Thomas Coke having been ordained by Wesley a bishop, and Richard Whatcoat and Thomas Vasey elders, for the purpose of consecrating Francis Asbury a bishop over the new Church, and of ordaining other preachers to the orders of elder and deacon, that the sacraments might be administered among the scattered Societies. A system of government, with its Liturgy, Articles of Re-

* Compare Appendix, Table No. III, with the Minutes.

ligion, Discipline, Hymn Book, etc., was formally adopted, and the denomination thus took precedence, in its episcopal organization, of the Protestant Episcopal Church in the United States. Its bishops were the first Protestant bishops of the western hemisphere.

In 1785 Freeborn Garrettson extended its labors to the northeastern British Provinces; in 1789 Jesse Lee extended them into the New England States; and in 1790 William Losee extended them into Upper Canada. In New England it was destined to become the second religious denomination in numerical strength and the first in progress, reporting in our day about a hundred thousand members, nearly a thousand preachers, at least one academy for each of its conferences, a university, and a theological school. In Canada it was destined to raise up many mighty evangelists, to keep pace with emigration, and reach westward to the Pacific, and eastward till it should blend with the Methodism planted by Coughlan, M'Geary, Black, and Garrettson on the Atlantic coast; Indian missions were to arise; Methodist chapels, many of them elegant structures, to adorn the country; a Book Concern, periodical organs, a university, and academies be provided; and Methodism, as in the United States, to become numerically the predominant faith of the people apart from the Church of England; its different branches* reporting in our day more than a hundred thousand members and nearly one thousand traveling preachers.

Before the end of the century Methodism had planted its standards from Nova Scotia to Georgia, from the Atlantic coast to the furthest western line of emigration. It ended the century with eight Annual Conferences, or Synods, with three bishops, Coke, Asbury, and Whatcoat, with two hundred and eighty-seven traveling preachers, besides hundreds of local preachers, and with nearly sixty-five thousand church members, of whom more than thirteen thousand were Africans. In the first Annual Conference, 1773, all the preachers save one, William Watters, were foreigners; but after the first General Conference (1784) Wesley dispatched no "missionaries" to America. All his former missionaries, except Asbury and Whatcoat, had returned to Europe, or located; but American Methodism had now its native ministry, numerous and vigorous. Besides Asbury, Coke, and Whatcoat, it still retained many of the great evangelists it had thus far raised up, Garrettson, Lee, Abbott, O'Kelly, Crawford, Burke, Poythress, Bruce, Breeze, Reed, Cooper, Everett, Willis, Dickins, Ware, Brush, Moriarty, Roberts, Hull, Losee, and others. A host of mighty men,

* The Canada and other Wesleyan Conferences, and the Methodist Episcopal and New Connection Churches.

who were yet young and obscure, had already joined these standard-bearers: M'Kendree, George, (both afterward bishops,) Roszel, Nolley, M'Gee, Smith, Gibson, M'Henry, Kobler, Fleming, Cook, Scott, Wells, Pickering, Sharp, Bostwick, M'Claskey, M'Combs, Bartine, Morrell, Sargent, Taylor, Hunt, and scores more. These were soon to be followed, or rather joined, by another host of as strong if not stronger representative men: Roberts, Hedding, Soule, Bangs, Merwin, Capers, Pierce, Winans, Kennon, Kenneday, Douglass, Redman, Thornton, Finley, Cartwright, and many others equal to them; and amid an army of such were to arise in due time, to give a new intellectual development to the ministry, such characters as Elliott, Ruter, Emory, Fisk, Summerfield, Bascom, Olin, and others, some surviving to our day, men of not only denominational but of national recognition.

The Church retained vividly the consciousness and spirit of its original mission as a revival of apostolic religion. Its ministry was remarkable for its unction and preached with demonstration and with power; its social and public worship was characterized by animation and energy; it was continually promoting "revivals" and "reformations," extending them, not only over conferences or single states, but sometimes simultaneously over much of the nation. Therefore was its growth rapid beyond parallel; the

65,000 members with which it began our century, had swelled by the year 1825 to nearly 350,000, its 287 preachers to more than 1,300.

By the year 1844, when it was divided by the secession of the South, it comprised more than 1,170,000 members, and more than 4,600 traveling preachers; it had gained, in the preceding four years, 430,897 members and 1,325 preachers, an average of 107,724 members and 331 preachers per year. Thus, in the hour of its most gigantic strength and capacity for usefulness, when its arms could be outstretched to the ends of the world with the blessings of the Gospel of peace, was the mighty Colossus broken in twain.

But the loyal Church fast recovered its strength and moved onward, so that by 1850 it reported nearly 690,000 members, 4,129 traveling and 5,420 local preachers. In 1860 it reported 994,447 members, 6,987 traveling and 8,188 local preachers; and the two bodies, North and South, enrolled 1,743,515 members, 9,771 traveling and 13,541 local preachers.

This hundredth year of the denomination witnesses in the Methodist Episcopal Church alone 60 conferences, 928,320 members, 6,821 itinerant preachers, 8,205 local preachers, 10,015 churches, valued, with their 2,948 parsonages, at $26,883,076.* Including both branches of Methodism, North and

* Minutes of 1864, the latest published before the present volume goes to press.

South, the aggregate is 1,628,388 members, 9,421 traveling, and 13,205 local preachers.* Its congregations are among the largest in the country, and its terms of Church membership are among the most stringent known in Protestant Christendom. It is a moderate calculation that there are three members of its congregations to one of its communicants, including its numerous children and youth; at this rate the aggregate population, more or less habitually under the influence of its two leading Churches, North and South, can hardly be less than 6,710,000; it is more likely about 7,000,000, more than one fifth of the population of the nation.

Adding the other branches of Methodism, there must now be in the United States 1,950,000 members and 12,000 traveling preachers religiously training, more or less, a population of 7,800,000 souls. In the whole western hemisphere, including the West Indies and British North America, there are at least 2,100,000 Methodists.

In the four Middle states, New York, Pennsylvania, New Jersey, and Delaware, "Methodism had in 1850, according to the United States census, 2,556 churches, while the four remaining evangelical and leading denominations—the Baptist, Congregationalists, Episcopalian, and Presbyterian—had an aggre-

* The latest Southern reports are for 1860. The war has doubtless affected them, as the above figures show it has Northern Methodism.

gate of only 3,600, showing that Methodism holds about three quarters of the popular power of evangelical Christianity in that central division of the country, where the leading state and the metropolitan city of the continent are found. In the ten Southern states and the District of Columbia, the above-named denominations have 4,458 churches, the Methodists 5,015, which gives Methodism an excess of several hundred churches over this combined evangelical competition; and in the eleven Western states, the comparison stands: the four denominations, 4,899 churches; Methodism, 4,863, which, with the statistics of the territories compiled since the census of 1850, will give to the youngest leading religious body in the land a relative ascendancy still greater than in the states of the South. The sum of it all is, that in New England, Methodism is rapidly gaining on the ancestral religion; that in the Middle states, it nearly balances the four great evangelical denominations; that in the states of the South, it more than balances them; that in the great West, which is soon to wield a weightier influence than all the other states combined, it has taken a still stronger position."*

* Tefft's Methodism, p. 199.

CHAPTER V.

ITS PRACTICAL SYSTEM.

The historical answer to the question, What is Methodism? is not complete without a more precise account of its practical or "Disciplinary" system.

The first organic form which the new movement took was that of the "United Society," founded by Wesley in connection with the "Old Foundry," London. The model of this elementary organization was before him in the Fetter Lane and other societies to which he had resorted in the metropolis. These Societies rapidly multiplied throughout the country. In their maturer form, they were composed of members, and probationers (six months on trial), divided into classes of twelve or more persons, and meeting weekly, under the care of a Class-leader, for religious counsel and the contribution of money for the support of the Church according to the General Rules. The leaders were met at first weekly, afterward monthly, by the preacher.

The Class Meeting became one of the most important institutions of Methodism: the basis of its financial economy and the germ of almost every new Society formed in its rapid progress. The two Wesleys prepared the document, known now throughout the Methodist world as "The General Rules," and prescribing the "only one condition previously required of those who desire admission into these Societies."* It is distinguished by its practical thoroughness, and, equally, by the absence of any dogmatic requisitions. As presenting the "only" terms of membership in the Church, it is a striking proof of what we have assumed to be the stand-point, the providential design of Methodism, namely, the revival and propagation of spiritual religion; not of sectarian ecclesiasticism, or sectarian theology.

Each Society has its Trustees, holding the chapel property; its Stewards, having charge of its other finances; and, in many cases, its licensed Exhorters and Local Preachers, men who pursue secular vocations, but labor as public teachers whenever they find opportunity. The Exhorters usually graduate to the office of Local Preacher, and thence to the traveling ministry; this, in fine, is the recruiting process of the Annual Conference. Each Society also has its "Prayer Meetings," in which its lay talents, without respect to sex, are brought into exercise, and thereby developed and made subservient to the common cause; its Love-Feasts, derived through the Moravians, from the primitive Agapæ, and held usually

* See it in Appendix No. 1.

once a quarter; its Watch-nights, generally celebrated on the last night of the year.

A group of these Societies form a Circuit, extending in some cases five hundred miles, requiring from two to six or more weeks to travel around it, and supplied by a preacher "in charge," and two or three assistants, who are aided by the Local Preachers; the Class-Leaders maintaining a minute pastoral oversight of the Societies during the absence of the itinerants.

A group of circuits constitute a District, superintended by a Presiding Elder, who incessantly travels his extensive territory, preaching, counseling the traveling and Local Preachers and Exhorters, meeting the official members of the circuit Societies, and promoting the interest of the Church in every possible way.

The Quarterly Conference is held by the Presiding Elder, in accordance with its title, once in three months, on each circuit, and is composed of the preachers of the circuit, its local preachers, exhorters, leaders, stewards, and Sunday-school superintendents. It has, subordinately to the Annual Conference, jurisdiction over all the local interests of the circuit: its finances, the authorization of its local preachers and exhorters, a class of judicial appeals, and the recommendation of candidates for the Annual Conferences. Formerly its exercises were largely, mostly indeed, spiritual. It continued about two days, during which there were almost continual sessions, sermons, prayer-meetings, or love-feasts. The Methodist families of the circuit, often from the distance of many miles, assembled at it, making it a great religious festival.

A number of districts (with their Quarterly Conferences) constitute the Annual Conference, composed of the traveling preachers of the given territory. These annual assemblies became imposing occasions. A bishop presided; the preachers, from many miles around, usually including several states, were present; hosts of laymen were spectators. There was preaching in the early morning, in the afternoon, and at night. The daily proceedings were introduced with religious services, and were characterized by an impressive religious spirit. They continued usually a week, and it was a festal season, gathering the war-worn heroes of many distant and hard-fought fields, renewing the intimacies of preachers and people, and crowned alike by social hospitalities and joyous devotions. They have their particular regulations prescribed in the Discipline.

All the Annual Conferences are represented by delegates in the General Conference, which meets once in four years, and is the supreme assembly of the denomination, making its "rules and regulations," under certain Restrictive Rules, and revising its whole work and interests. Its session usually lasts about four weeks; it is the great jubilee of the denomination, and has unquestionably become one of the most important ecclesiastical occasions of the Christian world.

Such is a mere glance at the "economy" or practical system of Methodism, not altogether as it was under Wesley in England, but as it developed and enlarged itself in America at and after the Christmas General Conference of 1784, when the Church assumed an organic form with its series of synodal bodies, extending from the fourth of a year to four years, from the local circuit to the whole nation; its series of pastoral functionaries, Class-leaders, Exhorters, Local Preachers, Circuit Preachers, District Preachers or Presiding Elders, and Bishops whose common diocese was the entire country; its Prayer-meetings, Band-meetings, Love-feasts, and incessant preaching; its Ritual, Articles of Religion, Psalmody, and singularly minute moral discipline, as prescribed in its "General Rules" and ministerial regimen. Its system was remarkably precise and consecutive, and, as seen in our day by its results, as remarkably effective. Time has proved it to be the most efficient of all modern religious organizations, not only among the dispersed population of a new country, but also in the dense communities of an ancient people; on the American frontier, and in the English city, it is found efficacious beyond all other ecclesiastical plans, stimulating most others, and yet outstripping them. This singular system of religious instrumentalities was not devised. It was in but few respects the result of sagacious foresight; it grew up spontaneously, and Wesley's legislative wisdom shows itself not so much in inventing its peculiarities, as in appropriating skillfully the means which were providentially provided for him. Its elementary parts were evolved unexpectedly in the progress of the denomination. Wesley saw that the state of religion throughout the English nation required a thorough reform; God, he believed, would provide for whatever was necessary to be done in such a necessity, if willing and earnest men would attempt to do it. He was ready to attempt it, and to be sacrificed for it. He looked not into the future, but consulted only the openings of his present duty. He expected at first to keep within the restrictions of the national Church. The manner in which he was providentially led to adopt, one by one, the peculiar measures which at last consolidated into a distinct and unparalleled system, is an interesting feature in the history of Methodism, and worthy to be traced with more particular attention than we have hitherto been able to give it.

The doctrines which he preached, and the novel emphasis with which he preached them, led to his expulsion from the pulpits of the Establishment. This treatment, together with the great assemblies he attracted, compelled him to preach them *in the open air:* a measure which the moral wants of the country demanded, and which is justified, as well by the example of Christ as by its unquestionable results.

The inconvenience of the "room" occupied by his followers for spiritual meetings at Bristol, led to the erection of a more commodious edifice. This was a place of occasional preaching, and finally, without the slightest anticipation of such a result, the first in *a series of chapels* which became the habitual resorts of his followers, and thereby contributed more, perhaps, than any other cause to their organization into a distinct sect. The debt incurred by this building rendered necessary *a plan of pecuniary contributions* among the worshipers who assembled in it. They agreed to pay a penny a week. They were divided into companies of twelve, one of whom, called the leader, was appointed to receive their pittances. At their weekly meetings, for the payment of this contribution, they found leisure for religious conversation and prayer. These companies, formed only for a local and temporary object, were afterward called *classes*, and the arrangement was incorporated into the permanent economy of Methodism. In this manner originated one of the most distinctive features of its system, the advantages of which are beyond estimation. The class-meeting has, more than any other means, preserved the original purity and vigor of the denomination. It is the best school of experimental divinity that the world has seen in modern times. It has given a sociality of spirit and a disciplinary training to Methodism which have been characteristic of it, if not peculiar to it.

We cannot but admire the providential adaptation of this institution to another which was subsequently to become all-important in the Methodist economy— an *itinerant ministry*. Such a ministry could not admit of much local pastoral labor, especially in the New World, where the circuits were long. The class-leader became a substitute for the preacher in this department of his office. The fruits of an itinerant ministry must have disappeared in many, perhaps most, places during the long intervals which elapsed between the visits of the earlier preachers, had they not been preserved by the class-meeting.

Another most important result of the class-meeting was the pecuniary provision it afforded for the prosecution of the plans which were daily enlarging under the hands of Wesley. The whole *fiscal system* of Methodism arose from the Bristol penny collections, modified at last into the "rule" of "a penny a week and a shilling a quarter." Thus, without foreseeing the great independent cause he was about to establish, Wesley formed, through a slight circumstance, a simple and yet most effective system of finance for the expenses which its future prosecution would involve. And admirably was this pecuniary system adapted to the circumstances of that cause. He was destined to raise up a great religious organization; it was to be composed chiefly of the poor, and yet to require large pecuniary resources. How were these resources to be provided from among a poor people? The providential formation of a plan of finance which suited the poverty of the poorest, and which worldly sagacity would have contemned, banished all difficulty, and has led to pecuniary results which have rarely if ever been equaled by any voluntary religious organization.

The itinerant lay ministry was equally providential in its origin. Wesley was at first opposed to the employment of lay preachers. He expected the co-operation of the regular clergy. They, however, were his most persistent antagonists. Meanwhile the small societies, formed by his followers for spiritual improvement, multiplied. "What," he says, "was to be done in a case of such extreme necessity, where so many souls lay at stake? No clergyman would assist at all. The expedient that remained was to seek some one among themselves who was upright of heart and of sound judgment in the things of God, and desire him to meet the rest as often as he could, to confirm them, as he was able, in the ways of God, either by reading to them or by prayer and exhortation." From exhortation these men proceeded to exposition, from exposition to preaching. The result was natural, but it was not designed. Such was the origin of the Methodist *lay ministry.*

The multiplication of societies exceeded the increase of preachers. It thus became necessary that the lat ter should travel from town to town, and thence arose the *itinerancy*, one of the most important features of the ministerial system of Methodism. It is not a labor-saving provision—quite the contrary—but a laborer-saving one. The pastoral service, which would otherwise have been confined to a single parish, was extended by this plan to scores of towns and villages, and, by the co-operation of the class-meeting, was rendered almost as efficient as it would have been were it local. It was this peculiarity that rendered the ministry of Methodism so successful in new countries. It also contributed, perhaps more than any other cause, to maintain a sentiment of unity among its people. It gave a pilgrim, a militant character to its preachers; they felt that "here they had no abiding city," and were led more earnestly to seek one out of sight. It would not allow them to entangle themselves with local trammels. The cross peculiarly "crucified them to the world, and the world to them." Their zeal, rising into religious chivalry; their devotion to one work; their disregard for ease and the conveniences of stationary life, were owing largely to their itinerancy. It made them one of the most self-sacrificing, laborious, practical, and successful bodies of men which have appeared in the great field of modern Christian labor. And it was the opinion of Wesley that the time when itinerancy should cease in the ministry, and classes among the laity of Methodism, would be the date of its downfall.

These developments inevitably led to others. It was necessary that Wesley should advise his preachers; they met him annually for the purpose, and from such informal consultations arose the constitutional *Conference*, a body whose title has taken a prominent place in the ecclesiastical terminology of Christendom, among the names of councils, convocations, and synods. Its deliberations at last originated the laws, defined the theology, and planned the propagandism of the denomination. Its Minutes, revised and reduced, became the *Methodist Discipline.* It has reproduced itself in Ireland, in France and Germany, in the American Republic, in the British North American Provinces, in Australia, in India and in Africa; and it promises to be a perpetually if not a universally recognized institution of the Protestant world.

With the erection of churches arose the necessity

for the appointment of *Trustees* to hold their property. The finances of the societies rendered necessary the appointment of local *Stewards;* the multiplication of societies, the appointment of *Circuit Stewards*, to whom the local stewards became auxiliaries. The increase of business on the circuits led to the creation of the *Quarterly Meeting*, or Quarterly Conference as it is called in America, comprising the officers, lay and clerical, of the several societies of the circuit; and the *District Meeting* or Conference, combining several circuits. And thus, wheel within wheel, the system took form, and became a settled and powerful economy.

The importance of this system becomes still more striking when we consider its adaptation to the New World—to the immense fields of immigration and civilization which were about to be opened in not only North America, but in Oceanica, the "Island World," to which geographers give rank as the fifth division of the globe, and along whose now busy coasts Cook, the navigator, was furtively sailing while Wesley was founding Methodism in England. Its importance to our own country will be considered hereafter.

It has been objected to the ecclesiastical system of Methodism that it excludes its laity from its higher councils. Historically this fact is not discreditable to it. Its early preachers went forth not at the call of the people, but to call the people. A small body of ecclesiastics, they traversed the land preaching and forming Societies on circuits hundreds of miles long. These Societies were usually feeble, individually; they were composed mostly of poor, dispersed, and unlettered people; and the preachers were compelled to have the almost exclusive management of their scattered, untrained Churches. It was necessary for the itinerants to meet periodically to revise and rearrange their labors; these periodical assemblies were called, as we have seen, by the unpretentious name of Conferences; it would have been impossible, in the early days of the denomination, to have gathered, in their sessions, any satisfactory lay representation of the Societies. The conference grew into the supreme legislature and judiciary of the Church, and thus came to pass, at last, the startling anomaly of the largest religious body in the republic, a body, too, entirely pervaded by the republican sentiments of the country, yet controlled exclusively, in at least its higher assemblies, by its clergy. The fact was not the result of design, it was historically an accident, and I repeat, in nowise dishonorable to the ministry. In agitations for a reform of this fact, there has been no little contention and confusion, but opposition to a change has not arisen so much from theories of church government, as from a fear, on the part of loyal laymen and preachers, that the practical efficiency of the system would be endangered by any radical change. Theories of Church polity have been of course more or less unavoidable in such discussions, but practical expediency has been the main question with both parties. The liberality, not to say liberalism, of Methodism in theology (hereafter to be shown) has characterized it equally in matters of Church government. It does not admit that there is any scriptural or divinely enjoined form of ecclesiastical polity, but that practical expedience is the only divine right of any system. Its own system is essentially Presbyterian, a Presbyterian episcopacy. Its bishop is a presbyter in "order," though a bishop in office; a presbyter superintending the body of presbyters, *primus inter pares.* In retaining the two clerical orders of presbyter and deacon, it does not declare that they are necessary to the validity of the ministry, nor impeach sister Churches that have them not; in adopting ordination, by imposition of hands, it does not assert any sacramental virtue or scriptural obligation in the rite, but uses it as an impressive and appropriate ceremony. In America Methodism has always, since its organization, had bishops, in England it has never had them; in America it has the two orders of the ministry, in England it has but one; in the former it has always practiced "ordination" by imposition of hands, in England it never used such ordination until some years ago, when it was adopted at the suggestion of an American visitor, and solely as an expedient form; and yet British and American Methodism have never questioned each others' scriptural validity.

Basing all Church government on Christian expediency, American Methodism is ready for any modifications of its system which time may show to be desirable for its greater effectiveness. Its General Conference has therefore formally declared that it is not only willing to provide for lay representation whenever the Churches demand it, but that it approves of the change. Many Annual Conferences have also formally seconded this declaration of the supreme body, and it is evident that the Church is now generally becoming convinced that in its present maturity it can safely modify its government in this respect, and thus rid itself of an ecclesiastical anomaly which, if it has not seriously interfered with its prosperity, has at least been a disparagement to its character, especially in the writings of its opponents. Lay representation is a prospective, apparently a certain fact of American Methodism, and with it will come, it may be hoped, a reunion of most if not all its various sects in the nation, this being now the only important question between most of them and the parent body.

CHAPTER VI.

ITS DOCTRINAL SYSTEM.

It has been affirmed that, consistently with its Providential mission, as a revival of spiritual life in Christendom, Methodism did not start on its career with any new dogmas, or any sectarian or theological exclusiveness. It has its theology nevertheless, and this theology has doubtless been one of the most potent elements of its vitality as an ecclesiastical movement. Not a single doctrine, however, did it announce, or does it yet proclaim, that was not sanctioned by the standards of the Anglican establishment. It was not, as we have seen, novelty of opinion so much as the earnestness with which Methodism uttered the acknowledged doctrines of the Church, that gave offense and provoked opposition and proscription. Wesley provided the theology of American Methodism in a symbol called the "Articles of Religion," and these articles were taken from the "Thirty-nine Articles" of the Anglican Church. They are abridged, and in some cases slightly amended, but they convey no tenet which is not received by the Church of England, and they are the only officially recognized standard of Methodist doctrine in America. Wesley's emendations chiefly guard them against interpretations favorable to sacramental regeneration and other Romish errors.

Singularly enough, the opinions which are considered most distinctive of Wesleyan theology have no expression in the "Articles of Religion," which, by Wesley's own prescription, have become the dogmatic standard of American Methodism. He eliminates the supposed Anglican Calvinism, but he does not introduce his own Arminianism, except in the thirty-first Anglican article on the "Oblation of Christ," which is Arminian as to the extent of the atonement. In like manner we have no statement of his doctrines of the "Witness of the Spirit" and "Christian Perfection." And yet no doctrines more thoroughly permeate the preaching, or more entirely characterize the moral life of Methodism than his opinions of the universal salvability of men, assurance, and sanctification. He evidently designed the articles to be the briefest and barest possible symbol of expedient doctrines; and, as we shall hereafter see, not even a requisite condition of Church membership, though a requisite functional qualification for the ministry. He consigned his other tenets, however precious to him, to other means of conservation and diffusion, for it was not his opinion that the orthodoxy of a Church can best guarantee its spiritual life, but rather that its spiritual life can best guarantee its orthodoxy.

The Arminianism of Wesley has been rightly so called. It is essentially true to the teachings of the great theologian of Holland, though not to the elaborations of his system by Episcopius and Limborch, and much less to the perversions of its later eminent representatives. Wesley had the courage to place the name of Arminius on his periodical organ, one of the earliest and now the oldest of religious magazines in the Protestant world. His Arminianism was far from being that mongrel system of semi-Pelagianism and semi-Socinianism which, for generations, was denounced by New England theologians as Arminianism, until the most erudite Calvinistic authority of the eastern states (Prof. Stuart of Andover) rebuked the baseless charge and bade his brethren be no longer guilty of it. Wesley taught "original sin" in the language of the ninth Anglican Article; though he taught also that both the justice and mercy of the Creator require that the human race should not have been continued, under this law of hereditary depravation, unless adequate provision were made for it by the atonement; he preached, therefore, universal redemption. He taught with the tenth Anglican article, on "Free Will," that "the condition of man, after the fall of Adam, is such that he cannot turn and prepare himself, by his natural strength and works, to faith and calling upon God;" that he has "no power to do good works, pleasant and acceptable to God, without the grace of God, by Christ, preventing" him; but he taught also that such "preventing grace" is provided for all responsible souls, and that none could be responsible without it. With the eleventh Anglican article he taught "justification by faith" alone, "and not for our own works and deservings;" yet he also taught that "good works follow after justification," and "do spring out, necessarily, of a true and lively faith." He taught the absolute sovereignty of God: that, like the potter with the clay, he can make some vessels for more, some for less honor; yet he also taught that, as wisdom and beneficence are essential attributes of the divine sovereignty, God neither would nor could (any more than the wise potter with his clay) make some for the gratification of a wanton caprice in their destruction, much less in their interminable anguish.

Of Wesley's Doctrine of Assurance, founded upon the text, "The Spirit itself beareth witness with our spirits that we are the children of God," and upon analogous Scripture passages, I have already said that it was not a peculiar opinion of Methodism, but common, in its essential form, to the leading bodies of Christendom, Greek, Roman, and Protestant; that as a high theological as well as philosophical authority of our times, Sir William Hamilton, has declared, "Assurance was long universally held in the Protestant communities to be the criterion and condition of a true or saving faith; Luther declares, 'He who hath not assurance spews faith out;' and Melanchthon, that 'assurance is the discriminating line of Christianity from heathenism;' that assurance is indeed the *punctum saliens* of Luther's system, and unacquaintance with this, his great central doctrine, is one prime cause of the chronic misrepresentation which runs through our recent histories of Luther and the Reformation; that assurance is no less strenuously maintained by Calvin, is held even by Arminius, and stands essentially part and parcel of all the confessions of all Churches of the Reformation down to the Westminster Assembly." Wesley defines the doctrine clearly. "By the testimony of the Spirit," he says, "I mean an inward impression on the soul, whereby the Spirit of God immediately and directly witnesses to my spirit that I am a child of God; that Jesus Christ hath loved me, and given himself for me; that all my sins are blotted out, and I, even I, am reconciled to God. I do not mean hereby that the Spirit of God testifies this by any outward voice; no, nor always by an inward voice, although he may do this sometimes. Neither do I suppose that he always applies to the heart (though he often may) one or more texts of Scripture; but he so works upon the soul by his immediate influence, and by a strong, though inexplicable operation, that the stormy wind and troubled waves subside, and there is a sweet calm, the heart resting in Jesus, and the sinner being clearly satisfied that all his iniquities are forgiven and his sins covered." He disclaims any originality in his teachings on the subject, and says, "With regard to the assurance of faith, I apprehend that the whole Christian Church in the first centuries enjoyed it. For though we have few points of doctrine explicitly taught in the small remains of the ante-Nicene fathers, yet, I think, none that carefully read Clemens Romanus, Ignatius, Polycarp, Origen, or any other of them, can doubt whether either the writer himself possessed it, or all whom he mentions, as real Christians. And I really conceive, both from the *Harmonia Confessionum*, and whatever else I have occasionally read, that all reformed Churches in Europe did once believe, 'Every true Christian has the divine evidence of his being in favor with God.'" "I know likewise that Luther, Melanchthon, and many other (if not all) of the reformers, frequently and strongly assert that every believer is conscious of his own acceptance with God, and that by a supernatural evidence."

For his doctrine of Sanctification, Wesley adopted the title of "Perfection," because he found it so used in the Holy Scriptures. Paul and John he deemed sufficient authorities for the use of an epithet which he knew, however, would be liable to the cavils of criticism. The Christian world had also largely recognized the term in the writings of Clemens Alexandrinus, Macarius, Kempis, Fenelon, Lucas, and other writers, Papal and Protestant. Besides incessant allusions to the doctrine in his general writings, Wesley has left an elaborate treatise on it. Fletcher of Madeley, an example as well as an authority of the doctrine, published an essay on it, proving it to be scriptural as well as sanctioned by the best theological writers. Wesley's theory of the doctrine is precise and intelligible, though often distorted into perplexing difficulties by both its advocates and opponents. He taught not absolute, nor angelic, nor Adamic, but "Christian perfection." Each sphere of being has its own normal limits; God alone has absolute perfection; the angels have a perfection of their own above that of humanity, at least of the humanity of our own sphere; unfallen man, represented by Adam, occupied a peculiar sphere in the divine economy, with its own relations to the divine government, its own "perfection," called by Wesley Adamic Perfection; fallen, but regenerated man, has also his peculiar sphere as a subject of the Mediatorial Economy, and the highest practicable virtue (whatever it may be) in that sphere is its "perfection," is Christian perfection.

Admitting such a theory of perfection, the most important question has respect to its practical limit. When can it be said of a Christian man that he is thus perfect? Wesley taught that perfect Christians "are not free from ignorance, no, nor from mistake. We are no more to expect any man to be infallible than to be omniscient. . . . From infirmities none are perfectly freed till their spirits return to God; neither can we expect, till then, to be wholly freed from temptation; for 'the servant is not above his Master.' Neither in this sense is there any absolute perfection on earth. There is no perfection of degrees, none which does not admit of a continual increase. . . . The proposition which I will hold is this: 'Any person may be cleansed from all sinful tempers, and yet need the atoning blood.' For what? for 'negligences and ignorances;' for both words and actions, (as well as omissions,) which are, in a sense, transgressions of the perfect law. And I believe no one is clear of these till he lays down this corruptible body." Perfection, as defined by Wesley, is not then perfection, according to the absolute moral law; it is perfection according to the special remedial economy introduced by the Atonement, in which the heart, being sanctified, fulfills the law by love, (Rom. xii, 8, 10,) and its involuntary imperfections are provided for, by that economy, without the imputation of guilt, as in the case of infancy and all irresponsible persons. The only question, then, can be, Is it possible for good men to so love God that all their conduct, inward and outward, shall be swayed by love? that even their involuntary defects shall be swayed by it? Is there such a thing as the inspired writer calls the "perfect love" which "casteth out fear?" (1 John iv, 18.) Wesley believed that there is; that it is the privilege of all saints; and that it is to be attained by faith. "I want you to be *all love*," he wrote. "This is the perfection I believe and teach; and this perfection is consistent with a thousand nervous disorders, which that high-strained perfection is not. Indeed, my judgment is, that (in this case particularly) to overdo is to undo; and that to set perfection too high is the most effectual way of driving it out of the world." "Man," he says, "in his present state, can no more attain Adamic than angelic perfection. The perfection of which man is capable, while he dwells in a corruptible body, is the complying with that kind command, 'My son, give me thy heart!' It is the loving the Lord his God with all his heart, and with all his soul, and with all his mind." Such is his much misrepresented doctrine of Christian perfection. Wesley taught that this sanctification is usually gradual, but may be instantaneous;

as, like justification, it is to be received by faith.

Such are the theological characteristics of Methodism. It demands the assent of all its adult candidates for baptism to the Apostles' creed, and has in its Articles a general, though a very brief, platform, consisting of the leading dogmas of the universal Church; aside from these, it preaches, especially, Universal Redemption, Assurance, and Perfection. The latter are special to it, not so much as opinions, (for they are still, more or less, common to the Christian world,) but by the special emphasis with which Methodism utters them. They are the staple ideas of its preaching, of its literature, of its colloquial inquiries in its class-meetings, prayer-meetings, and in the Christian intercourse of its social life. Though the success of the denomination cannot be explained apart from its disciplinary system and its spiritual energy, yet unquestionably its spiritual life and its practical system could not long subsist without its special theology.

I have remarked on the striking fact that Wesley did not insert in the theological Articles of American Methodism the tenets which are deemed most distinctively Wesleyan, and which unquestionably have been a chief source of vitality to the denomination; but a still more singular fact remains to be noticed, namely: that he makes no theological opinions requisite for membership in the Church, and recognises no creed but the universal symbol of the early Church, the Apostles' creed, and this only in the administration of baptism. Of few things connected with Methodism does Wesley speak oftener or with more devout gratulation than of its catholicity. "One circumstance," he says, "is quite peculiar to the people called Methodists; that is, the terms upon which any persons may be admitted into their Society. They do not impose, in order to their admission, any opinions whatever. Let them hold particular or general redemption, absolute or conditional decrees. . . . They think, and let think. One condition, and one only, is required, a real desire to save their souls. Where this is, it is enough; they desire no more; they lay stress upon nothing else; they ask only, 'Is thy heart herein as my heart? If it be, give me thy hand.'" "Is there," he adds, "any other Society in Great Britain or Ireland that is so remote from bigotry? that is so truly of a catholic spirit? so ready to admit all serious persons without distinction? Where is there such another society in Europe? in the habitable world? I know none. Let any man show it me that can. Till then let no one talk of the bigotry of the Methodists." When he was in his eighty-fifth year, preaching in Glasgow, he wrote: "I subjoined a short account of Methodism, particularly insisting on the circumstance, there is no other religious society under heaven which requires nothing of men, in order to their admission into it, but a desire to save their souls. Look all round you; you cannot be admitted into the Church, or Society of the Presbyterians, Anabaptists, Quakers, or any others, unless you hold the same opinions with them, and adhere to the same mode of worship. The Methodists alone do not insist on your holding this or that opinion. . . . Now, I do not know any other religious society, either ancient or modern, wherein such liberty of conscience is now allowed, or has been allowed since the age of the Apostles. Here is our glorying, and a glorying peculiar to us. What society shares it with us?" The possible results of such liberality were once discussed in the Conference. Wesley conclusively determined the debate by remarking: "I have no more right to object to a man for holding a different opinion from me, than I have to differ with a man because he wears a wig and I wear my own hair; but if he takes his wig off, and begins to shake the powder about my eyes, I shall consider it my duty to get quit of him as soon as possible." "Is a man," he writes, "a believer in Jesus Christ? and is his life suitable to his profession? are not only the main, but the sole inquiries I make in order to his admission into our Society." Did he design the new American Church to be equally liberal? As the "General Rules," used in England, were retained, after the Christmas Conference, in America, as the "only one condition" of membership, and the "Articles of Religion" are not mentioned in these Rules, but placed apart in the Discipline, are not the Articles to be considered rather as an indicatory than an obligatory dogmatic symbol; an indication to sincere men, seeking an asylum for Christian communion, of what kind of teaching they must expect in the new Church, but not of what they would be required to avow by subscription?

The Articles and the General Rules are both parts of the organic or constitutional law of American Methodism, though the General Rules prescribe the "only condition" of membership, without an allusion to the Articles. Conformity to the doctrines of the Church is required by its statute law as a functional qualification for the ministry; but Church members cannot be excluded for personal opinions while their lives conform to the practical discipline of the Church; they can be tried and expelled for "sowing dissensions in the Societies by inveighing against their doctrines or discipline;" that is, in other words, not for their opinions, but for their moral conduct respecting their opinions. They cannot be expelled for anything short of defects which "are sufficient to exclude a person from the kingdom of grace and glory." And at what would Wesley himself have more revolted than the assumption that opinions, not affecting the Christian conduct of a member of his Society, were "sufficient to exclude him from the kingdom of grace and glory?"* This interesting historical fact is full of significance, as an example of that distinction between indicatory and obligatory standards of theological belief which Methodism has, perhaps, had the honor of first

* Such, it will scarcely be questioned, is the right of communion possessed by a person already in the Methodist Episcopal Church; but it has sometimes been a question whether doctrinal opinions are not required for admission by the administrative prescription adopted since Wesley's day, (Discipline, Part I, chap. 2, § 2): "Let none be received until they shall, on examination by the minister in charge before the Church, give satisfactory assurances both of the correctness of their faith and their willingness to keep the rules." It may be replied, 1. That, according to Wesley's definition of the faith, essential to a true Church, there could be no difficulty here. 2. That, as the requisition is merely an administrative one for the preachers, and prescribes not what are to be "satisfactory assurances," etc., the latter are evidently left to the discretion of the pastor, and the requirement is designed to afford him the opportunity of further instructing the candidate, or of receiving from him pledges that his opinions shall not become a practical abuse in the society. 3. If the rule amounts to more than this, it would probably be pronounced, by good judges of Methodist law, incompatible with the usages and general system of Methodism, an oversight of the General Conference which enacted it, and contrary to the General Rules, as guarded by the Restrictive Rules. 4. It would be a singular and inconsistent fact, that opinions should be made a condition of admission to the Church, but not of responsibility (except in their practical abuse) with persons already *in* the Church. (See History of the Religious Movement, etc., vol. ii, p. 443.)

exemplifying among the leading Churches of the modern Christian world.*

* See Articles of Religion, Appendix II Wesley's liberality would startle many Methodists of our day. I add a few examples: "This in Scripture, perhaps *not once in the sense we now use it.*" Notes term, (converted,) so common in modern writings, very rarely occurs on the New Testament, Acts iii, 19. "True *repentance is a change from spiritual death to spiritual life*, and leads to life everlasting." Acts xi, 18. "He that, first, reverences God, etc.; secondly, from this awful regard to him, not only avoids all known evil, but endeavors, according to the best light he has, to do all things well, is accepted of Him—through Christ, though he knows him not. The assertion is express, *and admits of no exception.* He is in the favor of God, *whether enjoying his written word and ordinances or not.*" Acts x, 35. "A mystic, who denies justification by faith (Mr. Law for instance) may be saved. But if so, what becomes of *Articulus stantus vel cadentis Ecclesiæ?* If so, is it not high time?

Projicere ampullas et sesquipedalia verba,

and to return to the plain word; 'He that feareth God and worketh righteousness is accepted with him?'" Journal, December 1st, 1767. "I have not for many years thought a consciousness of acceptance to be essential to justifying faith." A.D. 1768, vol. vii, p. 495. He published for the edification of his people the Life of one of the most active Unitarians of his day, and in the Preface remarks: "I was exceedingly struck at reading the following Life: having long settled it in my mind that the entertaining wrong notions concerning the Trinity was inconsistent with real piety. *But I cannot argue against matter of fact.* I dare not deny that Mr. Firmin was a pious man, although his notions of the Trinity were quite erroneous." Vol. vii, p. 574. "Who are we that we should withstand God? Particularly by laying down rules of Christian communion which exclude any whom he has admitted into the Church of the first-born from worshiping God together. O that all Church governors would consider how bold an usurpation this is on the authority of the supreme Lord of the Church! O that the sin of thus withstanding God may not be laid to the charge of those, *who perhaps with a good intention,*

Methodism has naturally, in the first century of its history, not developed largely in the way of systematic divinity. But it has a thorough and able doctrinal exposition in the "Theological Institutes" of Richard Watson, of whom Prof. J. W. Alexander, of Princeton College, says: "Turretine is, in theology, *instar omnium:* that is, so far forth as Blackstone is in law. Making due allowance for the difference of age, Watson, the Methodist, is the only systematizer, within my knowledge, who approaches the same eminence; of whom I use Addison's words: 'He reasons like Paley, and descants like Hall.'" Another systematic work is now in progress in the German language, from the pen of Prof. Warren;* one of the most important contributions from an American hand to modern theological literature. This author has endeavored to determine the true relative position of Methodist theology, and says: "There are four great complete Christo-theological systems, the contrarieties of which are so fundamental and exhaustive that every writer on sys-

but in an over fondness for their own forms, have done it, and are continually doing it!" Notes, Acts xi, 17. In fine he expresses his whole policy, as an ecclesiastical leader, in a letter to a friend: "The first of your particular advice is 'to keep in view the interests of Christ's Church in general, and of practical religion; not considering the Church of England, or cause of Methodism, but as subordinate thereto.' This advice I have punctually observed."

* Systematische Theologie, einheitlich behandelt. Von William F. Warren. Bremen, 1865.

tematic theology who is not willing to give up the essence of Christianity itself must, in respect to them, choose and maintain a definite stand-point. The four mentioned great systems of doctrine are the Roman Catholic, the Calvinistic, the Lutheran, and the Wesleyan. These systems rest on different conceptions of the soteriological relation of God and man as established by Christ, and correspond to different stages of development of the religious consciousness. Besides these four great systems there is no other worthy of notice. The Greek Church has as yet formed no definite regular system of doctrine, and, so long as she retains her present views, can form none which can radically differ from Romanism. The Church of England has, much less, a peculiar complete system. Her theology is a mass of the most discordant elements. Her books of doctrine are appealed to by Calvinists and Arminians, Puritans and Puseyites, Evangelicals and Sacramentarians, High and Low Churchmen, and with about equal propriety. If she is less one-sided than the Reformed and Lutheran Churches, nevertheless her teaching embraces almost all the incompleteness and errors of them both."

"According to the Roman Catholic view of Christianity, salvation is imparted through the (Papal) Church alone, and is conditioned on a meritorious co-working of the subject with grace. With this ground-view all the other peculiarities of the system, as, for example, the doctrine of the infallibility of the Church, priestly power, the merit of works, the sacrifice of the mass, purgatory, picture-worship, indulgences, angel and saint-reverencing, etc., are closely connected. According to its inmost spirit and essence, Catholicism is nothing other than an essentially pagan view of Christian truth.

"According to the Calvinistic view of Christianity, the salvation or non-salvation of each human being depends absolutely on the free action of God toward him. God, according to this system, has elected to certain salvation a certain unalterable number of mankind, accurately fixed before the foundation of the world, and has either predestinated all others to certain damnation, or within himself resolved to permit them, unredeemed, to perish in their inherited depravity. This eternal twofold decree he executes unfailingly in time through his gracious sovereignty. With this ground-view of Calvinism, all its other peculiarities, for example, its limited (partial) atonement, its total denial of human freedom, its dogma of the irresistibility of grace and of the impossibility of apostasy, are intimately connected. According to its inmost spirit and essence, this system is a conception of Christianity from the stand-point of an Old Testament faith.

"According to the Lutheran view of the soteriological relation of God and man, the salvation or non-salvation of each human being is solely dependent on his own personal action in regard to the means of grace, (the word and the sacraments.) If any one uses these properly, and everybody is capable of doing this through his own natural powers, then God will give to him, through these means of grace, faith, and with faith justification. If he continues diligently in the proper use of the word and of the sacraments, he will retain the received blessings and finally overcome death and hell. With this ground-view of Lutheranism, all the other peculiarities of the system, such as the bodily presence of Christ in the eucharist, the relative over-estimation of the sacraments, over-attachment to the Church, etc., are closely allied. In respect to its inmost spirit and essence this creed is a view of Christianity from the stand-point of justification.

"According to the Methodistic view of the soteriological relation of God and man, the salvation or non-salvation of each human being depends on his own free action in respect to the enlightening, renewing, and sanctifying inworkings of the Holy Spirit. If, in respect to these inworkings, he holds himself receptively, then will he become holy both here and hereafter; but if he closes his heart against the same, he will continue in death both here and in eternity. With this ground-view, all the other peculiarities of Methodism, such as its peculiar dogma of freedom, its emphasis of the working of the Holy Spirit, its doctrines of Christian perfection, etc., are intimately connected. In respect to its inmost spirit and essence it is a viewing of Christianity from the stand-point of Christian perfection or perfect love.

"Such is the stand-point, such the doctrinal and historical significance, of the Methodistic system. It presents Christian theology 'high as the love of God, deep as the want of man.' It is the ripe final result of the millennial-long spiritual study and searching of the Church of Christ into the truths of the divine revelation. And as soon as this view of the soteriological relation of God and man shall find universal prevalence and acceptance, so soon will the salvation or non-salvation of the soul cease to be made dependent either on human conduct in regard to a particular priesthood or an eternal decree of God, or on the mysterious working of Church ceremonies, but will be regarded as depending on man's own action in regard to the enlightening, renewing, and sanctifying influences of the Holy Spirit. Let us venture to hope for an early dawn of that day, so much anticipated and so anxiously wished for by so many and such earnest spirits of our time, in which a new and rich outgushing of the Holy Ghost will put an end to the intolerable disagreements of the old Churches and creeds, and reveal the kingdom of God in power and great majesty."

Such, then, is Methodism, as seen in its History, its Practical Economy, and its Theological Platform—a system of spiritual life, of Evangelical liberalism, of apostolic propagandism. As such it has pre-eminent claims on the consideration and gratitude of our age; but these claims it has further demonstrated by its beneficent, its extraordinary results, especially in this new world. We are now prepared to consider some of these results.

PART II.

WHAT HAS METHODISM ACHIEVED, ENTITLING IT TO THE PROPOSED COMMEMORATION?

CHAPTER I.

ITS SPECIAL ADAPTATION TO THE COUNTRY.

METHODISM, it has been affirmed, was a specia. provision for the early religious wants of this nation. The Revolution opened the continent for rapid settlement by immigration. A movement of the peoples of the old world toward the new was to set in on a scale surpassing that of the northern hordes which overwhelmed the Roman Empire. Much of this incoming population was to be Roman Catholic, most of it low, if not semi-barbarous. Some extraordinary religious provision was requisite to meet and counteract its demoralizing influence on the country.

The growth of population was to transcend the most credulous anticipations. The one million and a quarter (including blacks) of 1750, the less than three millions of 1780, were to be nearly four millions in 1790; nearly five and a third millions in 1800; more than nine and a half millions in 1820; nearly thirteen millions in 1830. Thus far they were to increase nearly thirty-three and a half per cent. in each decade. Pensioners of the war of the Revolution were to live to see the "Far West" transferred from the valleys of Virginia, the eastern base of the Pennsylvania Alleghanies, and the center of New York, to the great deserts beyond the Mississippi; to see mighty states, enriching the world, flourish on the Pacific coast; and to read, in New York, news sent the same day from San Francisco. Men, a few at least, who lived when the population of the country was less than three millions, were to live when it should be thirty millions.

Methodism, with its "lay ministry" and its "itinerancy," could alone afford the ministrations of religion to this overflowing population; it was to lay the moral foundations of many of the great states of the West. The older Churches of the colonies could never have supplied them with "regular" or educated pastors in any proportion to their rapid settlement. Methodism met this necessity in a manner that should command the national gratitude. It was to become at last the dominant popular faith of the country, with its standard planted in every city, town, and almost every village of the land. Moving in the van of emigration, it was to supply, with the means of religion, the frontiers from the Canadas to the Gulf of Mexico, from Puget's Sound to the Gulf of California. It was to do this indispensable work by means peculiar to itself; by districting the land into circuits which, from one hundred to five hundred miles in extent, could each be statedly supplied with religious instruction by one or two traveling evangelists who, preaching daily, could thus have charge of parishes comprising hundreds of miles and tens of thousands of souls. It was to raise up, without delay for preparatory training, and thrust out upon these circuits, thousands of such itinerants, tens of thousands of local or lay preachers and exhorters, as auxiliary and unpaid laborers, with many thousands of class-leaders who could maintain pastoral supervision over the infant societies in the absence of the itinerant preachers, the latter not having time to delay in any locality for much more than the public services of the pulpit. Over all these circuits it was to maintain the watchful jurisdiction of traveling presiding elders, and over the whole system the superintendence of traveling bishops, to whom the entire nation was to be a common diocese. It was to govern the whole field by Quarterly Conferences for each circuit, Annual Conferences for groups of circuits,

Quadrennial Conferences for all the Annual Conferences. It was to preach night and day in churches, where it could command them, in private houses, school-houses, court-houses, barns, in the fields, on the highways. It was to stud the continent with chapels, building them, in our times at least, at the rate of nearly two a day. It was to provide academies and colleges exceeding in number, if not in efficiency, those of any other religious body of the country, however older or richer. It was to scatter over the land cheap publications, all its itinerants being authorized agents for their sale, until its "Book Concern" should become the largest religious publishing house in the world. The best authority for the moral statistics of the country, himself of another denomination, (Dr. Baird,) was at last to "recognize in the Methodist economy, as well as in the zeal, the devoted piety and the efficiency of its ministry, one of the most powerful elements in the religious prosperity of the United States, as well as one of the firmest pillars of their civil and political institutions." The historian of the Republic (Bancroft) records that it has "welcomed the members of Wesley's Society as the pioneers of religion; that the breath of liberty has wafted their messages to the masses of the people; encouraged them to collect the white and negro, slave and master, in the green wood, for counsel on divine love and the full assurance of grace; and carried their consolation and songs and prayers to the furthest cabins in the wilderness."

It would indeed appear that the Methodist movement was thus a providential intervention for the new nation. As we have seen, it began its operations here at the dawn of the Revolutionary controversy; its infancy was cotemporaneous with the infancy of the Republic; it was the only form of religion that possessed much vitality or made any progress during the Revolutionary struggle; its denominational organization at the Christmas Conference anticipated the national organization under the Federal Constitution; it fairly started with the Republic, and has kept pace with it, establishing the ordinances of religion coextensively with the spread of the population and the laws of the Government. It not only, by its peculiar system, met the emergent moral necessities of the opening continent, but exerted also a most important influence on the other and older religious provisions of the land. Whitefield's repeated passages through the colonies had aroused the Churches for the coming wants of the country. The "Great Awakening" under Edwards, in New England, had subsided, and even reacted; Whitefield restored the evangelical vitality of New England, and it has never since been lost. The Presbyterian and Baptist Churches of the middle states were quickened into their subsequent and abiding energy by his flaming ministrations. The earliest religious impulses of the South were given by him. Methodism, organized, took up the work when he fell in the field, and it has never ceased to advance, in all evangelical denominations, beyond any foreign example. Methodism was not designed to supplant its elder sister Churches in the land, but to provoke them to new life and labors, while it accomplished its own given work. It nevertheless quickly surpassed them. We have authentic statistics of the leading Christian denominations of the United States for the first half of our century. They attest conclusively the peculiar adaptation of the ecclesiastical system of Methodism to the moral wants of the country. During the period from 1800 to 1850 the ratio of the increase of the ministry of the Protestant Episcopal Church has been as 6 to 1, of its communicants as 6 to 1; of the ministry of the Congregationalists as 4 to 1, of their communicants as $2\frac{2}{3}$ to 1; of the ministry of the regular Baptists as 4 to 1, of their communicants as $5\frac{2}{3}$ to 1; of the ministry of the Presbyterians ("old and new schools") as 14 to 1, of their communicants as $8\frac{1}{2}$ to 1; of the ministry of the Methodist Episcopal Church (North and South) as $19\frac{3}{8}$ to 1, of its communicants as $17\frac{3}{4}$ to 1. It must be borne in mind, however, that most if not all these religious bodies have, during the whole of this period, been more or less pervaded by the Methodistic impulse given by Whitefield and his successors, and much of their success is unquestionably attributable to that fact. Methodism has given them thousands of its converts and received but comparatively few from them.

CHAPTER II.

ITS LABORS FOR THE DIFFUSION OF LITERATURE.

METHODISM has always appreciated the importance of literature. If individual prejudices have seemed to indicate the contrary, they have been but exceptional to the general sentiment of the denomination. It began its march from the gates of a university. Wesley labored incessantly, by his pen, for the elevation of the popular mind. A German historian of Methodism classifies, with German elaborateness, the great variety of his literary works, as Poetical, Philological, Philosophical, Historical, and Theological. Though he wrote before Wesley's death, he states that many of these writings, after ten or twenty editions, could be obtained only with difficulty, and the whole could not be purchased for less than ten guineas, notwithstanding they were published at rates surprisingly cheap; for Wesley was the first to set the example of modern cheap prices sustained by large sales. A catalogue of his publications, printed about 1756, contains no less than one hundred and eighty-one articles in prose and verse, English and Latin, on grammar, logic, medicine, music, poetry, theology, and philosophy. Twc thirds of these publications were for sale at less than one shilling each, and more than one fourth at a penny. They were thus brought within reach of the poorest of his people. "Simplify religion and every part of learning," he wrote to Benson, who was the earliest of his lay preachers addicted to literary labors. To all his preachers he said, "See that every society is supplied with books, some of which ought to be in every house."

It has justly been said that Wesley reduced many folios and quartos to pocket volumes; he waded through the mass of the learned works of his day, and, simplifying, multiplying, cheapening them, presented in the cottages and hovels of the poor almost every variety of useful or entertaining knowledge. In addition to his own prose productions, constituting fourteen octavo volumes in the English edition and seven in the American, his "Notes" and abridgments make a catalogue of one hundred and eighteen prose works, (a single one of which, The Christian Library, contains fifty volumes,) forty-nine poetical publications by himself and his brother, and five distinct works on music. Not content with books and tracts, Wesley projected, in August, 1777, the Arminian Magazine, and issued the first number at the beginning of 1778. It was one of the first four religious magazines which sprung from the resuscitated religion of the age, and which began this species of periodical publications in the Protestant world. Though nominally devoted to the defense of the Arminian theology, it was miscellaneous in its contents, and served not only for the promotion of religious literature, but of general intelligence. He conducted it till his death, and made faithful use of it for the diffusion of knowledge among the people. It is now the oldest religious periodical in the world. It may be questioned whether any English writer of the last or the present century has equaled Wesley in the number of his productions.

American Methodism has always been true to this example of English Methodism, and in fact has far transcended it. Its "Book Concern" is now the largest religious publishing house in the world. As early as 1789, John Dickins, then the only Methodist preacher in Philadelphia, was appointed "Book Steward" of the denomination. The first volume issued by him was the "Christian Pattern," (Wesley's translation of Kempis's celebrated "Imitation;") the "Methodist Discipline," the "Hymn Book," "Wesley's Primitive Physic;" and reprints of the first volume of the "Arminian Magazine," and Baxter's "Saint's Rest," followed. The only capital of the Concern was about six hundred dollars, lent to it by Dickins himself. In 1790 portions of Fletcher's "Checks" were reprinted. In 1797 a "Book Committee" was appointed, to whom all books were to be submitted before their publication—a guardianship of its press which has ever since been maintained by the Church. In 1804 the Concern was removed from Philadelphia to the city of New York. It had early attempted the publication of a monthly magazine, in imitation of Wesley's periodical, but failed, till 1818, when the Methodist Magazine was begun; it still prosperously continues under the title of the Methodist Quarterly Review. In 1824 the Concern secured premises of its own on Crosby-street, with presses, bindery, etc. In 1823 the "Youth's Instructor," a monthly work, was begun. The same spirit of enterprise led to the publication of the Christian Advocate and Journal, which appeared, for the first time, on the 9th of September, 1826. The success of the Advocate was remarkable. "In a very short time," writes Dr. Bangs, one of its original publishers, "its number of subscribers far exceeded every other paper published in the United States, being about twenty-five thousand; and it soon increased to thirty thousand, and was probably read by more than one hundred and twenty thousand persons, young and old." It should be noticed, also, that, at the earnest request of Methodists west of the mountains, the General Conference of 1820 authorized the establishment of a branch of the Book Concern in Cincinnati, a precedent which led to secondary branches in various parts of the country. The rapid increase of the business very soon led to the necessity of enlarging its buildings. Accordingly all the vacant ground in Crosby-street was occupied. But even these additions were found insufficient to accommodate the several departments of labor, so as to furnish the supply of books, now in constantly increasing demand. To meet this deficiency five lots were purchased in Mulberry-street, between Broome and Spring streets, and one building erected in the rear for a printing office and bindery, and another of larger dimensions projected.

Soon after the General Conference of 1832, the agents began the erection of the front building on Mulberry-street; and in the month of September, 1833, the entire establishment was removed into the new buildings. In these commodious rooms, with efficient agents and editors at work, everything seemed to be going on prosperously, when suddenly in 1836 the entire property was consumed by fire. The Church thus lost not less than two hundred and fifty thousand dollars. The buildings, all the printing and binding materials, a vast quantity of books, bound and in sheets, a valuable library which the editor had been collecting for years, were in a few hours destroyed. Fortunately the "Concern" was not in debt. By hiring an office temporarily, and employing outside printers, the agents soon resumed their business, the smaller works were put to press, and "the Church's herald of the news, the Christian

Advocate and Journal, soon took its flight again (though the first number after the fire had its wings much shortened) through the symbolical heavens, carrying the tidings of our loss, and of the liberal and steady efforts which were making to reinvigorate the paralyzed Concern." At the General Conference of 1836 the plan of a new building was submitted and approved, and the agents entered upon their work with energy and perseverance. The new buildings went up with all convenient dispatch, in a much better style, more durable, better adapted to their use, and safer against fire than the former. The front edifice is one hundred and twenty-one feet in length and thirty in breadth, four stories high above the basement, with offices for the agents and clerks, a bookstore, committee rooms, etc. The building in the rear is sixty-five feet in length, thirty in breadth, and four stories high, and is used for stereotyping, printing, binding, etc.

In our day the Methodist Book Concern, aside from that of the Methodist Episcopal Church, South, which was founded by a division of its funds, comprises two branches, eastern and western, and seven depositories, with an aggregate capital of more than $837,000. Four "Book Agents," appointed by the General Conference, manage its business. It has twelve editors of its periodicals, nearly five hundred clerks and operatives, and between twenty and thirty cylinder and power presses constantly in operation. It publishes above five hundred "General Catalogue" bound books, besides many in the German and other languages, and about fifteen hundred Sunday-school volumes. Its Tract publications number about nine hundred in various tongues. Its periodicals are a mighty agency, including one Quarterly Review, four monthlies, one semi-monthly, and eight weeklies, with an aggregate circulation of over one million of copies per month. Its quarterly and some of its weeklies have a larger circulation than any other periodicals, of the same class, in the nation, probably in the world.

The influence of this great institution, in the diffusion of popular literature and the creation of a taste for reading among the great masses of the denomination, has been incalculable. It has scattered periodicals and books all over the valley of the Mississippi. Its sales in that great domain, in the quadrennial period ending with January 31, 1864, amounted to about $1,200,000. If Methodism had made no other contribution to the progress of knowledge and civilization in the New World than that of this powerful institution, this alone would suffice to vindicate its claim to the respect of the enlightened world. Its ministry has often been falsely disparaged as unfavorable to intelligence; but it should be borne in mind that its ministry founded this stupendous means of popular intelligence, and has continued to work it with an increasing success up to the present time. They have been, as we have seen, its salesmen; they have scattered its publications over their circuits. Wesley enjoined this service upon them in their Discipline. "Carry books with you on every round," he said; "leave no stone unturned in this work;" and thus have they spread knowledge in their courses over the whole land, and built up their unparalleled "Book Concern." There has never been an instance of defalcation on the part of its "Agents;" it has never failed in any of the financial revulsions of the country; and it is now able, by its large capital, to meet any new literary necessity of the denomination.

CHAPTER III.

ITS EDUCATIONAL EFFORTS.

CRADLED in a university, and trained by such men as the Wesleys, Fletcher, Benson, Coke, Clarke, Watson, Methodism could not be indifferent, much less hostile, to the education of the people, though its poverty, and its absorption in more directly moral labors for their elevation, did not at first allow much scope to its educational measures. Wesley, however, never lost sight of such measures; and it is an interesting fact, that in the year which is recognized as the epoch of Methodism, the date of its first field preaching, and among the miserable people where the latter began, it also began the first of its literary institutions. And if anything could enhance the interest of this fact, it is that the founders of both Methodistic parties, Calvinistic and Arminian, shared in the founding of the first Methodist seminary. Whitefield laid the corner-stone of the Kingswood School; and kneeling upon the ground, surrounded by reclaimed and weeping colliers, prayed that "the gates of hell" might not prevail against it; while the prostrate multitude, now awakened to a new intellectual as well as moral life, responded with hearty Amens. Wesley reared it by funds which he reserved from the income of his college fellowship or received from his followers. It was the germ of the later institution which bears its name, and which has become an educational asylum for the sons of itinerant preachers. Its accommodations were subsequently found to be insufficient for the growing numbers of such pupils, and the estate of "Woodhouse Grove," not far from Leeds, was purchased for a second institution of the same character. In our day from two hundred to two hundred and fifty sons of preachers and missionaries are educated within them, and gratuitously boarded and clothed during a term of six years. The Connection has expended between £300,000 and £400,000 upon these seminaries. Wesley also early projected schools for poor children at Newcastle and London. His preaching-house at the former place was called the Orphan-House, and its deed provided that it should maintain a school of forty poor children, with a master and mistress. Its site is now occupied by a substantial edifice for a Mixed and Infants' Wesleyan Day School, and also a Girls' Industrial School. More than four hundred children are daily receiving instruction within its walls. He maintained for years, also, a school at the Old Foundry.

As early as his first conference, in 1744, Wesley

proposed a theological school or "Seminary for Laborers." It could not then be attempted for want of funds. The project was reconsidered at the next session, and failed for the same reason. Kingswood School was made a kind of substitute for it, but the original design was never abandoned, and is embodied to-day in the two effective "Theological Institutions" of Richmond and Didsbury, and the two "Biblical Institutes" of American Methodism. Such were some of the efforts for education made by the Methodism of Wesley's day. They have since given origin to a system of educational provisions as extensive, if not as effective, as belongs to any other English or American Protestant body, except the Anglican and Scotch Establishments: to the Wesley College in Sheffield, the Collegiate Institution in Taunton, (both of them in a collegiate relation to the University of London,) the Wesleyan Normal Institution at Westminster, whose stately buildings cost $200,000, and accommodate more than one hundred students preparing to be teachers; to a grand scheme of Day Schools which at present comprises nearly five hundred schools and sixty thousand pupils.

American Methodism early shared this interest of the parent body in education. In the year of its formal organization (1784) Coke and Asbury projected the Cokesbury College, and laid its foundations the next year at Abingdon, twenty-five miles from Baltimore. In 1787 Asbury consecrated and opened it with public ceremonies. In 1795 it was destroyed by fire, but a second edifice was soon after secured in Baltimore; this, however, shared the fate of its predecessor. It has been supposed that these disasters not only discouraged Asbury, but led him fallaciously to infer that Providence designed not the denomination to devote its energy to education. It was far otherwise, however, with that great man; he no longer believed that collegiate or pretentious institutions of learning should be attempted by the Church while yet in its infancy, but he never abandoned the design of secondary or more practically adapted institutions. He formed, indeed a grand scheme, for the establishment of academies, all over the territory of the denomination. As far south as Georgia, contributions in land and tobacco were received for the purpose; and in the yet frontier settlements of Kentucky, such institutions were attempted under his auspices. At Bethel, Kentucky, an edifice and organization was really obtained, but financially broke down at last. In 1818 Dr. Samuel K. Jennings and other Methodists attempted a college in Baltimore, but this also failed. No failures, however, no discouragement, could obliterate from the mind of the denomination the conviction of its responsibility for the education of the increasing masses of its people. In 1820 the General Conference recommended that all the Annual Conferences should establish seminaries within their boundaries; thus proposing to supply the whole republic with such schools, though with considerable territorial intervals. This demonstration of interest for education, in the supreme body of the Church, was prompted by the spontaneous enterprise of the ministry and the people, who, three years before, had, chiefly under the guidance of Dr. Martin Ruter, started an institution in New England, (at New Market, N. H.,) still distinguished, in its later location, at Wilbraham, Mass., and in 1819 another, chiefly under the guidance of Dr. Nathan Bangs, in New York city, afterward transferred to White Plains, N. Y. The impulse thus given not only produced numerous academies, but led, in 1823, to the beginning of Augusta College, Ky., whose edifice was erected in 1825, and commenced the series of modern collegiate institutions under the patronage of the Church, so that by the General Conference of 1832, says the biographer of Hedding, Bishop Clark, "the Wesleyan University had been established at Middletown, Conn., and Dr. Wilbur Fisk, of the New England Conference, was at its head, and John M. Smith, of the New York Conference, one of the professors. Madison College, now extinct, but whose place has since been supplied by Alleghany College, had gone into successful operation, in Western Pennsylvania; J. H. Fielding had succeeded H. B. Bascom as president, and H. J. Clark was one of the professors; both were members of the Pittsburgh Conference. Augusta College had been established under the patronage of the Kentucky and Ohio Conferences; Martin Ruter was president, and H. B. Bascom, J. S. Tomlinson, J. P. Durbin, and Burr H. M'Cown, were professors; all of them members of the Kentucky Conference except J. P. Durbin, who belonged to the Ohio. In the south-west, Lagrange College had been established; Robert Paine was president, and E. D. Simms one of the professors. In Virginia, Randolph Macon College had been established, and M. P. Parks, of the Virginia Conference, was one of its professors, and Stephen Olin was soon after placed at its head. Thus it will be seen that no less than *five* colleges had sprung into existence in an incredibly short time, and were already in successful operation under the supervision of the Church. Several conference seminaries also had been established; such were the Cazenovia Seminary, the Maine Wesleyan Seminary, Wilbraham Academy, Genesee Wesleyan Seminary, Shelbyville Female Academy, and others, which were in successful operation in different parts of the Church."

The Church could not pause here. Wesley, as we have seen, had proposed ministerial education at his very first conference, and the British Methodists had embodied the proposition in two imposing "theological institutions." The New England Methodists agitated the question in their Church periodical, and in 1839 a convention was called, in Boston, to provide such an institution. It was founded with the title of the Biblical Institute; it struggled through severe adversities, was at first connected with the Wesleyan University, Middletown, Conn., then with the Methodist Seminary, at Newbury, Vt., but at last was located in Concord, N. H., where it has exerted no inconsiderable influence upon the character of the New England Methodist ministry. In 1845 the Rev. John Dempster, D. D., of New York city, became its professor of theology. He threw his remarkable energy into the cause of ministerial education throughout the denomination, and not only forced along the New England institution against formidable discouragements, but became a leading founder of the north-western seminary at Evanston, Ill., where a Chicago Methodist lady, by the gift of property amounting to $300,000, gave endowment and her name to the Garrett Biblical Institute.

Thus boarding academies, colleges, and theological seminaries, have rapidly grown up in the denomination till the Methodist Episcopal Church alone now reports no less than 25 colleges, (including theological schools,) having 158 instructors; 5,345 students; $3,055,861 endowments and other property; and 105,531 volumes in their libraries. It reports also 77 academies, with 556 instructors and 17,761 students, 10,462 of whom are females, making an aggregate of 102 institutions, with 714 instructors and 23,106 students. The Southern division of the denomination reported before the war 12 colleges and 77 academies, with 8,000 students, making an aggregate for the two bodies of 191 institutions and 31,106 students.

The moral and social influence, in England and America, of such a series of educational provisions, reaching from the first year of Methodism to our own day, must be incalculable; and could it point the world to no other monuments of its usefulness, these would suffice to establish its claims as one of the effective means of the moral progress of the English race in both hemispheres since Wesley began his singular career.*

* The limits of this work will not admit of more detail in these important facts. I give, however, a tabular view of Methodist educational institutions in the United States, as reported in 1865, in the Appendix No. IV.

CHAPTER IV.

ITS SUNDAY-SCHOOL ENTERPRISE.

METHODISM has an honorable place in the history of Sunday-schools. As early as 1769 a young Methodist, Hannah Ball, established a Sunday-school in Wycombe, England, and was instrumental in training many children in the knowledge of the Holy Scriptures. Doubtless similar attempts were made before that time, but they were only anticipations of the modern institution of Sunday-schools. In 1781, while another Methodist young woman (afterward the wife of the celebrated lay preacher, Samuel Bradburn,) was conversing in Gloucester with Robert Raikes, a benevolent citizen of that town and publisher of the Gloucester Journal, he pointed to groups of neglected children in the street, and asked: "What can we do for them?" She answered: "Let us teach them to read and take them to Church!" He immediately proceeded to try the suggestion, and the philanthropist and his female friend attended the first company of Sunday-scholars to the Church, exposed to the comments and laughter of the populace as they passed along the street with their ragged procession. Such was the origin of our present Sunday-school, an institution which has perhaps done more for the Church and the social improvement of Protestant communities than any other agency of modern times, the pulpit excepted. Raikes and his humble assistant conducted the experiment without ostentation. Not till November 3, 1783, did he refer to it in his public journal. In 1784 he published in that paper an account of his plan. This sketch immediately arrested the attention of Wesley, who inserted the entire article in the January number of the Arminian Magazine for 1785, and exhorted his people to adopt the new institution. "They took his advice," says an historian of Methodism, and "laboring, hard-working men and women began to instruct their neighbors' children, and to go with them to the house of God on the Lord's day." The same year, as we learn from a letter of Mary Fletcher, her husband, "lately hearing of Sunday-schools, thought much upon them, and then set about the work." He soon had three hundred children under instruction, and diligently trained them till his last illness. He drew up proposals for six such schools in Coalbrook Dale, Madeley, and Madeley Wood. He wrote an essay on "the Advantages likely to Arise from Sunday-Schools," and designed to prepare small publications for their use, but his death cut off his plans.

Wesley's earliest notice of Sunday-schools is in his

Journal for July 18, 1784, the year of Raikes's published account of them. He speaks of them prophet ically: "I find these schools springing up wherever I go; perhaps God may have a deeper end therein than men are aware of; who knows but some of these schools may be nurseries for Christians?" They were introduced into the metropolis by the Calvinistic Methodist, Rowland Hill, in 1786; and in the same year they were begun in the United States by the Methodist bishop, Francis Asbury, and this first Sunday-school of the New World prefigured one of the most important later advantages of the institution, by giving a useful preacher to the Methodist Episcopal Church. Wesley mentions in 1786, that five hundred and fifty children were taught in the Sunday-school of his society at Bolton, and the next year he found there eight hundred, taught by eighty "masters." Richard Rodda, one of his preachers, records that, in 1786, he formed a Sunday-school in Chester, and soon had nearly seven hundred children "under regular masters." Wesley wrote to him in the beginning of 1787: "I am glad you have taken in hand that blessed work of setting up Sunday-schools in Chester. It seems these will be *one great means of reviving religion throughout the nation.* I wonder Satan has not yet sent out some able champion against them." On the 18th of April, 1788, Wesley preached at Wigan "a sermon for the Sunday-schools," and "the people flocked from all quarters in a manner that never was seen before." The year before his death he wrote to Charles Atmore, an itinerant preacher: "I am glad you have set up Sunday-schools at Newcastle. This is one of the best institutions which has been seen in Europe for some centuries." Thus is Methodism historically connected with both the initiation and outspread of this important institution. Under the impulse of its zeal the Sunday-school was soon almost universally established in its societies. A similar interest for it prevailed among other religious bodies; and in three years after Raikes's published account of it, more than two hundred thousand children were receiving instruction from its thousands of teachers. The Irish Conference of 1794 voted: "Let Sunday-schools be established as far as possible in all the towns of this kingdom where we have societies;" and in March, 1798, a "Methodist Sunday-School Society" was formed at City Road Chapel, London. In the following December Drs. Coke and Whitehead preached the first sermons before it. In our day Methodism, exclusive of all minor sects which bear the name, has under its direction an army of nearly 500,000 scholars and more than 80,000 teachers in England and Scotland.

For many years American Methodism made no provision for the general organization or affiliation of its Sunday-schools. Its Book Concern issued some volumes suitable for their libraries, chiefly by the labors of Rev. Dr. Durbin, who prepared its first Library volume and its first Question Book; but no adequate, no systematic attention was given to this sort of literature. It was obvious, on a moment's reflection, that an almost illimitable field for the enlargement of the business of the Concern and the diffusion of useful knowledge was at its command in this direction. Accordingly the "Union" was organized on the 2d of April, 1827. Dr. Bangs says: "The measure indeed was very generally approved, and hailed with grateful delight by our friends and brethren throughout the country. It received the sanction of the several Annual Conferences, which recommended the people of their charge to form auxiliaries in every circuit and station, and send to the general depository in New York for their books; and such were the zeal and unanimity with which they entered into this work that at the first annual meeting of the society there were reported 251 auxiliaries, 1,025 schools, 2,048 superintendents, 10,290 teachers, and 63,240 scholars, besides above 2,000 managers and visitors. Never, therefore, did an institution go into operation under more favorable circumstances, or was hailed with a more universal joy, than the Sunday-School Union of the Methodist Episcopal Church." This great success, however, could not save it from the misfortunes of bad management. Under "an injudicious attempt," writes Dr. Bangs many years later, "to amalgamate the Bible, Tract, and Sunday-School Societies together, by which the business of these several societies might be transacted by one board of management," and by other causes, it declined, if indeed it did not fail, until resuscitated by the zeal of some New York Methodists and by an act of the General Conference of 1840. It passed through modifications till it assumed its present effective form of organization, and grew into colossal proportions under the labors of its indefatigable secretaries, Rev. Drs. Kidder and Wise. It now has (aside from its offspring in the Methodist Episcopal Church South) 13,400 schools, more than 150,000 teachers and officers, and near 918,000 scholars, about 19,000 of whom are reported as converted during the last year. There are in the libraries of these schools more than 2,529,000 volumes. They are supported at an annual expense of more than $216,000, besides nearly $18,000 given to the Union for the assistance of poor schools. There are circulated among them semi-monthly nearly 260,000 "Sunday-School Advocates," the juvenile periodical of the Union. The numbers of conversions among pupils of the schools, as reported for the last eighteen years, amounts to more than 285,000, showing that much of the extraordinary growth of the

Church is attributable to this mighty agency. The Union has four periodicals for teachers and scholars, two in English and two in German, and their aggregate circulation is nearly 300,000 per number. Its catalogue of Sunday-school books comprises more than 2,300 different works, of which more than a million of copies are issued annually. Including other issues, it has nearly 2,500 publications adapted to the use of Sunday-schools. In fine, few if any institutions of American Methodism wield a mightier power than its Sunday-School Union.

CHAPTER V.

ITS MISSIONARY LABORS.

A DISTINGUISHED English writer, a layman of the Church of England, has said that "the Methodism of the last century, even when considered apart from its consequences, must always be thought worthy of the most serious regard: that, in fact, that great religious movement has, immediately or remotely, so given an impulse to Christian feeling and profession, on all sides, that it has come to present itself as the starting-point of our modern religious history; that the field-preaching of Wesley and Whitefield, in 1739, was the event whence the religious epoch, now current, must date its commencement; that back to the events of that time must we look, necessarily, as often as we seek to trace to its source what is most characteristic of the present time; and that yet this is not all, for the Methodism of the past age points forward to the next-coming development of the powers of the Gospel." *

These remarks are especially true in respect to the relation of Methodism to modern Christian Missions. The idea of religious Missions is as old as Chris-

* Isaac Taylor's Wesley and Methodism, Preface.

tianity, and has been exemplified by the Papal Church through much of its history and in the ends of the world. The Moravians early embodied it in their system. In the Protestantism of England it had but feeble sway till the epoch of Methodism. That sublime form of it which now characterizes English Protestantism in both hemispheres, and which proposes the evangelization of the whole race, appeared in the latter part of the eighteenth century. Societies for the propagation of the Gospel had previously existed in Great Britain, but they were provided chiefly, if not exclusively, for the Christianization of countries which, by reason of their political dependence upon England, were deemed to have special claims on British Christianity—the inhabitants of India and the Indians of North America. An historian of missions, writing in 1844, says: "It was not until almost within the last fifty years that the efforts of the religious bodies by whom Christian missions are now most vigorously supported were commenced." *

Methodism was essentially a missionary movement, domestic and foreign. It initiated not only the spirit, but the practical plans of modern English missions. Bishop Coke so represented the enterprise in his own person for many years as to supersede the necessity of any more formal organization of it, but it was none the less real and energetic. The historian

* Ellis's History of the London Missionary Society, vol. i, p. 3.

just cited says: "The Wesleyan Missionary Society was formed in 1817, but the first Wesleyan missionaries who went out, under the superintendence of the Rev. Dr. Coke, entered the British colonies in 1786. The Baptist Missionary Society was established in 1792; the London Missionary Society in 1795; and the Edinburgh or Scottish and the Glasgow Missionary Societies in 1796. The subject also engaged the attention of many pious persons belonging to the Established Church, besides those connected with the London Missionary Society, and by members of that communion the Church Missionary Society was organized in the first year of the present century." The London Missionary Society, embracing most Dissenting bodies of England, arose under the influence of Calvinistic Methodism, and the Church Missionary Society sprang from the evangelical Low Church party which Methodism, Calvinistic and Arminian, had originated in the Establishment, Venn, the son of the Methodist churchman Venn, being its projector.

Though Bishop Coke represented the Arminian-Methodist Mission interest, as its founder, secretary, treasurer, and collector, it really took a distinct form some six years before the formation of the first of the above named societies. Coke spent more than a year in bringing the Negro missions before the English people immediately after his second visit to the West Indies. In 1786 a formal address was issued to the public in behalf of a comprehensive scheme of Methodist missions. It was entitled "An Address to the Pious and Benevolent, proposing an Annual Subscription for the Support of Missionaries in the Highlands and adjacent Islands of Scotland, the Isles of Jersey, Guernsey, and Newfoundland, the West Indies, and the Provinces of Nova Scotia and Quebec. By Thomas Coke, LL.D. 1786." It speaks of "a mission intended to be established in the British dominions in Asia," but which was postponed till these more inviting fields should be occupied. This scheme was called in the address an "Institution;" it was really such; though not called a society, it was one in all essential respects; and if the fact that it was not an extra-ecclesiastical plan, but a part of the system of Methodism, should detract from its claim of precedence in respect to later institutions of the kind, that consideration would equally detract from the Moravian missions, which were conducted in a like manner. The Address filled several pages, and was prefaced by a letter from Wesley indorsing the whole plan.

The next year (1787) the Wesleyan Missions bore the distinctive title of "Missions established by the Methodist Society." At the last Conference attended by Wesley (1790) a Committee of nine preachers, of which Coke was chairman, was appointed to take charge of this new interest. Coke continued to conduct its chief business; but the committee were his standing council, and formed, in fact, a Mission Board of Managers two years before the organization of the first of British missionary societies. Collections had been taken in many of the circuits for the institution, and in 1793 the Conference formally ordered a general collection for it. Coke published accounts of its "receipts and disbursements." The amount for 1787 was £1,167. The names of eminent Churchmen, Dissenters, and Calvinistic as well as Arminian Methodists, are reported on its list of subscribers. Among them are those of Whitbread, Wilberforce, the Thorntons, the Earl of Dartmouth, Earl of Belvidere, Lord Elliott, Lady Mary Fitzgerald, Lady Maxwell, Sir Charles Middleton, (afterward Lord Barham,) Sir Richard Hill, Sir John Carter, Sir William Forbes, Lady Smythe, Hon. Mrs. Carteret, and the Hon. Mrs. Bouverie; the Rev. Mr. Dodwell, of Lincolnshire;* Melville Horne, of Madeley; Berridge, of Everton; Abdy, of Horsleydown; Dr. Gillies, of Glasgow; Simpson, of Macclesfield; Pentycross, of Wallingford; Easterbrook, of Bristol; Kennedy, of Teston, and others.

In this manner did Methodism early prompt the

* This clergyman (of the Establishment) several years afterward made a contribution of £10,000 to the Wesleyan Missionary Society.

British Churches, and call forth the energies of the British people, in plans of religious benevolence for the whole world. Its previous missions in Scotland, Wales, Ireland, and the Channel Islands did much for the reformation of the domestic population. Besides its efforts in 1786 in the West Indies, it began its evangelical labors in France as early as 1791, and its great schemes in Africa in 1811; in Asia in 1814; in Australasia in 1815; in Polynesia in 1822; until, from the first call of Wesley for American evangelists, in the Conference of 1769, down to our day, we see the grand enterprise reaching to the shores of Sweden, to Germany, France, and the Upper Alps; to Gibraltar, and Malta; to the banks of the Gambia, to Sierra Leone, and to the Gold Coast; to the Cape of Good Hope; to Ceylon, to India, and to China; to the Colonists and Aboriginal tribes of Australia; to New Zealand, and the Friendly and Fiji Islands; to the islands of the Western, as well as of the Southern Hemisphere; and from the Gulf of St. Lawrence to Puget's Sound. From 1803 to the present time Wesleyan Methodism has contributed more than twenty millions of dollars for foreign evangelization. In England the "Church Missionary Society" alone exceeds its annual collections for the foreign field; but the Wesleyan Society enrolls more communicants in its Mission Churches than all other British missionary societies combined. The historian of religion during the last and present centuries would find it difficult to point to a more magnificent monument of Christianity. Methodism, gathering its hosts mostly from the mines and cottages of England, has embodied them in this sublime movement for the redemption of the world. Its poor have kept its treasury full. They have supplied hundreds if not thousands of their sons and daughters as evangelists to the heathen; and while they have thus been enabled to do good in the extremities of the earth, they have reaped still greater good from the reacting influence of their liberality upon themselves. They have received from it the sentiment of self-respect which comes from well-doing. They have been led to habits of frugality that their poverty might be consecrated by liberality. They have been elevated above the perversion of local or personal sentiments, by sympathies with their whole race. They have been led to a knowledge of the geography of the world, and to habits of reflection upon its religious, social, and political interests, by the habitual reading of missionary intelligence. They have been brought into closer social as well as Christian communion with one another by their frequent missionary meetings. Thousands of them have acquired habits of public usefulness by the management of their missionary affairs; and sentiments of universal philanthropy and religious heroism have been spread through their ranks to ennoble their own souls while saving the souls of others.

Coke, the first bishop of American Methodism, the first Protestant bishop of the new world, was to the end of his life the representative character of Methodist Missions. In his old age he offered himself to the British Conference as a missionary to the East Indies; he died on the voyage, and was buried in the Indian Ocean. His death struck not only a knell through the Church, but a summons for it to rise universally and march around the world. He had long entertained the idea of universal evangelization as the exponent characteristic of the Methodist movement. The influence of the movement on English Protestantism had tended to such a result, for in both England and America nearly all denominations had felt the power of the great revival, not only during the days of Whitefield and Wesley, but ever since. Anglo-Saxon Christianity, in both hemispheres, had been quickened into new life, and had experienced a change amounting to a moral revolution. The sublime apostolic idea of evangelization in all the earth, and till all the earth should be Christianized, had not only been restored, as a practical conviction, but had become pervasive and dominant in the consciousness of the Churches, and was manifestly thenceforward to shape the religious history of the Protestant world. The great fermentation of the mind of the civilized nations—the resurrection, as it may be called, of popular thought and power—cotemporaneous in the civil and religious worlds, in the former by the American and French Revolutions, in the latter by the Methodist movement, seemed to presage a new history of the human race. And history is compelled to record, with the frankest admission of the characteristic defects of Thomas Coke, that no man, not excepting Wesley or Whitefield, more completely represented the religious significance of those eventful times.

Though American Methodism was many years without a distinct missionary organization, it was owing to the fact that its whole Church organization was essentially a missionary scheme. It was, in fine, the great Home Mission enterprise of the north American continent, and its domestic work demanded all its resources of men and money. It early began, however, special labors among the aborigines and slaves. The history of some of these labors would be an exceedingly interesting and even romantic record, but our limits admit but this passing allusion to them. The year 1819 is memorable as the epoch of the formal organization of its missionary work. Dr. Nathan Bangs, long distinguished as its secretary and chief representative, was also its chief founder. He made it the theme of much preliminary conversation with his colleagues and the principal Methodist laymen of New York city. Rev. Dr. Laban Clark introduced it by a resolution to the attention of the metropolitan preachers at their weekly meeting, "consisting," says Dr. Bangs, "of Freeborn Garrettson, Samuel Merwin, Laban Clark, Samuel Howe, Seth Crowell, Thomas Thorp, Joshua Soule, Thomas Mason, and myself. After an interchange of thoughts the resolution was adopted, and Garrettson, Clark, and myself were appointed a committee to draft a constitution. When this committee met we agreed to write, each, a constitution, then come together, compare them, and adopt the one which should be considered the most suitable. The one prepared by myself was adopted, submitted to the Preachers' Meeting, and, after some slight verbal alterations, was finally approved. We then agreed to call a public meeting in the Forsyth-street Church on the evening of the 5th of April, 1819, which was accordingly done. I was called to the chair, and after the reading of the constitution Joshua Soule moved its adoption, and supported his motion by a powerful speech, concluding by an appeal to the people to come forward and subscribe it. He was seconded by Freeborn Garrettson, who also plead in favor of the scheme, from his own experience in the itinerant field from Virginia to Nova Scotia." The constitution was unanimously adopted, and the following officers were chosen: Bishop M'Kendree, President; Bishops George and Roberts, and Nathan Bangs, Vice-Presidents; Thomas Mason, Corresponding Secretary; Joshua Soule, Treasurer; Francis Hall, Clerk; Daniel Ayres, Recording Secretary. The following managers were also chosen: Joseph Smith, Robert Mathison, Joseph Sanford, George Suckley, Samuel L. Waldo, Stephen Dando, Samuel B. Harper, Lancaster S. Burling, William Duval, Paul Hick, John Westfield, Thomas Roby, Benjamin Disbrow, James B. Gascoigne, William A. Mercein, Philip J. Arcularius, James B. Oakley, George Caines, Dr. Seaman, Dr. Gregory, John Boyd, M. H. Smith, Nathaniel Jarvis, Robert Snow, Andrew Mercein, Joseph Moses, John Paradise, William Myers, William B. Skidmore, Nicholas Schureman, James Wood, Abraham Paul. The historian of the society (Dr. Strickland) says: "It is obvious that almost its entire business was conducted by Dr. Bangs for many years. In addition to writing the constitution, the address and circular, he was the author of every Annual Report, with but one exception, from the organization of the society down to the year 1841, a period of twenty-two years. He filled the offices of Corresponding Secretary and Treasurer for sixteen years, without a salary or compensation of any kind, until his appointment to the first named office by the General Conference of 1836. That he has contributed more than any other man living to give character to our missionary operations, by the productions of his pen and his laborious personal efforts, is a well authenticated fact, which the history of the Church fully attests." In this single instance of his manifold public life he was to be identified with a grand religious history. He was to see the annual receipts of the Society enlarged from the $823 of its first year to $250,374, (including its offspring of the Methodist Episcopal Church, South, to half a million,) and its total receipts, down to the last year of his life, more than four and a half millions, not including the southern Society. He was to witness the rise (chiefly under the auspices of the Society) of American-German Methodism, an epochal fact in the history of his Church, next in importance to the founding of the Church by Embury and Strawbridge. Without a missionary for some time after its origin, the Society was to present to his dying gaze a list of nearly four hundred missionaries and more than thirty-three thousand mission communicants, representing the denomination in many parts of the United States, in Norway, Sweden, Germany, Switzerland, Bulgaria, Africa, India, China, and South America. Assisting in this great work, and rejoicing in its triumphs, he was to outlive all its original officers but three, Joshua Soule, Francis Hall, and Daniel Ayres: and all its original managers save three, Dr. Seaman, James B. Oakley, and William B. Skidmore.

The next General Conference, in 1820, sanctioned the scheme. Dr. Emory submitted an elaborate report on the subject. After reasoning at length upon it, he asked, "Can *we*, then, be listless to the cause of missions? We cannot. Methodism itself is a missionary system. Yield the missionary spirit, and you yield the very life-blood of the cause. In missionary efforts our British brethren are before us. We congratulate them on their zeal and their success. But your committee beg leave to entreat this Conference to emulate their example." The Conference adopted, with some emendations, the constitution prepared for the Society by Dr. Bangs. He thus saw his great favorite measure incorporated, it may be hoped forever, into the structure of the Church. He writes: "These doings of the Conference in relation to the Missionary Society exerted a most favorable influence upon the cause, and tended mightily to remove the unfounded objections which existed in some minds against this organization."

By the session of the General Conference of 1832, the Society's operations had extended through the states and territories of the nation, and had become a powerful auxiliary of the itinerant system of the Church. Hitherto it had been prosecuted as a domestic scheme, comprehending the frontier circuits, the slaves, the free colored people, and the Indian tribes; it had achieved great success in this wide field, and was now strong enough to reach abroad to other lands. It proposed, with the sanction of this Conference, to plant its standard on the coast of Africa, and send agents to Mexico and South America to ascertain the possibility of missions in those countries. Thus were begun those foreign operations of the Society which have since become its most interesting labors.

Its domestic Indian missions had now become numerous, and some of them were remarkably prosperous; "attended," Dr. Bangs says, "with unparalleled success." In Upper Canada they numbered, in 1831, no less than ten stations and nearly two thousand Indians "under religious instruction, most of whom were members of the Church. Among the Cherokees, in Georgia, they had at the same date no less than seventeen missionary laborers, and nearly a thousand Church-members. Among the Choctaws there were about four thousand communicants, embracing all the principal men of the nation, their chiefs and captains." And, more or less, along the whole frontier, Indian Missions were established. Meanwhile the destitute fields of the domestic work proper were dotted with humble but effective mission stations, from the St. Lawrence to the Gulf of Mexico, and these stations were rapidly passing from the missionary list to the Conference catalogue of appointments as self-supporting Churches.

In 1832 Melville B. Cox sailed for Africa, the first foreign missionary of American Methodism. He organized the Liberia Mission. He fell a martyr to the climate, but laid on that benighted continent the foundations of the Church, never, it may be hoped, to be shaken. The next year a delegation from the distant Flathead Indians of Oregon arrived in the states soliciting missionaries. Their appeal was zealously urged through the Christian Advocate, and received an enthusiastic response from the Church. Dr. Bangs, who had been a leading promoter of the African Mission, now, in co-operation with Dr. Wilbur Fisk, advocated this new claim with his utmost ability. Jason and Daniel Lee, and Cyrus Shepard, were dispatched as missionaries in the spring of 1834. An extraordinary scheme of labors was adopted, involving great expense; but, writes Dr. Bangs, "the projection of this important mission had a most happy effect upon the missionary cause generally. As the entire funds of the Society up to this time had not exceeded eighteen thousand dollars a year, and as this mission must necessarily cost considerable, with a view to augment the pecuniary resources of the Society, a loud and urgent call was made, through the columns of the Christian Advocate and Journal, on the friends of missions to 'come up to the help of the Lord' in this emergency; and to assist in this benevolent work, the Messrs. Lee were instructed, while remaining in the civilized world, to travel as extensively as possible, hold missionary meetings, and take up collections. The 'Flathead' Mission, as it was then called, seemed to possess a charm, around which clustered the warm affections of all the friends of the missionary enterprise, and special donations for the 'Flatheads' were sent to the treasury with cheering liberality and avidity. As an evidence of the beneficial result of these movements, the amount of available funds had risen, in 1834, from $17,097 05, the sum raised in 1833, to $35,700 15. So true is it that those who aim at great things, if they do not fully realize their hopes, will yet accomplish much."

The surges of emigration have overwhelmed nearly all that grand transmontane region; the aborigines are sinking out of sight beneath them; but the Oregon Mission, after some useful labors among the Indians, became the nucleus of the Christianity and civilization of the new and important state which has since arisen on the North Pacific coast.

Meanwhile Fountain C. Pitts was sent on the mission of inquiry to South America. In the autumn of 1835 he visited Rio Janeiro, Buenos Ayres, Monte Video, and other places, and the Methodist South American Mission was founded the next year by

Justin Spaulding. Thus had the Church borne at last its victorious banner into the field of foreign missions. It was to be tried severely in these new contests, but to march on through triumphs and defeats till it should take foremost rank among denominations devoted to foreign evangelization.

At the General Conference of 1836, it was found that the missionary cause had grown rapidly since the preceding session. In the last single year its receipts surpassed those of any preceding year by about twenty-two thousand dollars; and in the various missionary stations there had been within the same time an accession to the membership of the Church of more than four thousand converts. The Liberia Mission was now organized into an Annual Conference, and the operations of the Missionary Society had assumed such importance, and involved such responsibility, as to justify, in the judgment of the Conference, the appointment of a special officer, or "Resident Corresponding Secretary," who could devote his whole attention to them. Of course the mind of the Conference, as indeed of the general Church, turned spontaneously to Dr. Bangs as the man for such an office, and he was elected by a majority which surpassed that of any of the three bishops, or any of the numerous editors and Book Agents (save one of the latter) who were elected by ballot at this session.

At the adjournment of the Conference he returned to New York, and entered with energy upon his new functions. The first year of his secretaryship (1836–7) was signalized by the first recognition and announcement, by the Missionary Society, of one of the most remarkable events in the history of modern missions, the beginning of the German Methodist Missions. Professor Nast, a young German scholar of thorough but Rationalistic education, had been reclaimed by Methodism to the faith of the Reformation. In 1835 he was sent to labor among his countrymen in Cincinnati; in 1836 he was appointed by the Ohio Conference to a German charge on the Columbus District, comprising a circuit of three hundred miles and twenty-two appointments. Thus originated the most successful, if not the most important of Methodist missions; and in the next Annual Report of the Society the "German Mission," and the name of "William Nast," its founder and missionary, were first declared to the general Church. German Methodism rapidly extended through the nation, to Boston in the north-east, to New Orleans in the south-west. German Methodist Churches, circuits, districts, were organized. "In the brief space of fourteen years," says the historian of Methodist Missions, "the German Missions have extended all over the country, yielding seven thousand Church members, thirty local preachers, eighty-three regular mission circuits and stations, and one hundred and eight missionaries. One hundred churches were built for German worship, and forty parsonages. The increase in membership during the past year (1848) was nearly one thousand. Primitive Methodism appears to have revived in the zeal and simplicity and self-sacrificing devotion of the German Methodists. May they ever retain this spirit! No agency has ever been employed so specifically adapted to effect the conversion of Romanists as that which is immediately connected with the German Mission enterprise. The pastoral visitations of the preachers bringing them into immediate contact with German Catholics, their distribution of Bibles and tracts, their plain, pointed, and practical mode of preaching, all combine to bring the truth to bear upon that portion of the population; and the result is the conversion of hundreds from the errors of Romanism." The chief importance of the German Mission has, however, been developed since this date. It has not only raised up a mighty evangelical provision for the host of German emigrants to the New World, but under the labors of Dr. Jacoby, it has intrenched itself in the German "fatherland," and is laying broad foundations for a European German Methodism. German Societies and circuits, a German Conference, a German "Book Concern" and German periodicals, and a Ministerial

School, with all the other customary appliances of evangelical Churches, have been established; and, in our day, this Teutonic Methodism comprises, on both sides of the Atlantic, nearly thirty thousand communicants, and nearly three hundred missionaries.

It is impossible here to trace in detail the further outspread of this great interest, especially under the successful administration, since 1850, of its present secretary, Dr. Durbin, nor is it requisite to the plan of the present volume. Suffice it to say that the annual receipts of the Society which, the year before his administration began, amounted to about $104,000, have risen to nearly $560,000, and that besides its very extensive domestic work, the Methodist Episcopal Church has now missions in China, India, Africa, Bulgaria, Germany, Switzerland, Denmark, Norway, Sweden, and South America. Its Missions, foreign and domestic, have 1,059 circuits and stations, 1,128 paid laborers, (preachers and assistants,) and 105,675 communicants. The funds contributed to its treasury, from the beginning down to 1865, amount to about $6,000,000. About 350 of the missionaries preach in the German and Scandinavian languages, and more than 30,000 of the communicants are German and Scandinavian. The Methodist Episcopal Church, South, had before the rebellion missions in China, among the foreign settlers in the United States, among the American Indians, and the southern slaves. About three hund red and sixty of its preachers were enrolled as missionaries.

American, like British Methodism, has become thoroughly imbued with the apostolic idea of foreign and universal evangelization. With both bodies it is no longer an incidental or secondary attribute, but is inwrought into their organic ecclesiastical systems. It has deepened and widened till it has become the great characteristic of modern Methodism, raising it from a revival of vital Protestantism, chiefly among the Anglo-Saxon race, to a world-wide system of christianization, which has reacted on all the great interests of its Anglo-Saxon field, has energized and ennobled most of its other characteristics, and would seem to pledge to it a universal and perpetual sway in the earth. Taken in connection with the London and Church Missionary Societies, the British and Foreign Bible Society, the London Tract Society, to all of which Methodism gave the originating impulse, and the Sunday-school institution, which it was the first to adopt as an agency of the Church, it is not too much to say that it has been transforming the character of English Protestantism and the moral prospects of the world. Its missionary development has preserved its primitive energy. According to the usual history of religious bodies, if not indeed by a law of the human mind, its early heroic character would have passed away by its domestic success and the cessation of the novelty and trials of its early circumstances; but by throwing itself out upon all the world, and especially upon the worst citadels of paganism, it has perpetuated its original militant spirit, and opened for itself a heroic career, which need end only with the universal triumph of Christianity. English Methodism was considered, at the death of its founder, a marvelous fact in British history; but to-day the Wesleyan missions alone comprise more than twice the number of the regular preachers enrolled in the English Minutes in the year of Wesley's death, and nearly twice as many communicants as the Minutes then reported from all parts of the world which had been reached by Methodism. The latest reported number of Missionary communicants in the Methodist Episcopal Church equals nearly one half the whole membership of the Church in 1819, the year in which the missionary Society was founded, and is nearly double the membership with which the denomination closed the last century, after more than thirty years of labors and struggles.

CHAPTER VI.

ITS LOYALTY AND PATRIOTIC SERVICES.

THE first American missionaries of Wesley, being native Englishmen, and uncommitted to politics, left the country (all except Dempster, Asbury, and Whatcoat) at the outbreak of the Revolution. The infant Church therefore suffered for some time under the suspicion of disloyalty. The imputation was, however, unfounded. Methodism included no larger proportion of "Toryism" than any other denomination of the times, in the middle states, to which it was yet limited. Wesley, however, strengthened this suspicion by publishing an abridgment of his friend Dr. Johnson's "Taxation No Tyranny," under the title of "A Calm Address to the American Colonies," recommending loyalty to the crown. It is due to Wesley, nevertheless, to say that, by the time the war really began, he took sides with the Americans. The very next day after the arrival in England of the news of the battles of Lexington and Concord, he wrote to Lord North and the Earl of Dartmouth, severally, an emphatic letter. "I am," he said, "a High-Churchman, the son of a High-Churchman, bred up from my childhood in the highest notions of passive obedience and non-resistance, and yet, in spite of all my long-rooted prejudices, I cannot avoid thinking these, an oppressed people, asked for nothing more than their legal rights, and that in the most modest and inoffensive manner that the nature of the thing would allow. But waiving this, I ask, Is it common sense to use force toward the Americans? Whatever has been affirmed, these men will not be frightened, and they will not be conquered easily. Some of our valiant officers say that 'two thousand men will clear America of these rebels.' No, nor twenty thousand, be they rebels or not, nor perhaps treble that number. They are strong; they are valiant; they are one and all enthusiasts, enthusiasts for liberty, calm, deliberate enthusiasts. In a short time they will understand discipline as well as their assailants. But you are informed 'they are divided among themselves.' So was poor Rehoboam informed concerning the ten tribes; so was Philip informed concerning the people of the Netherlands. No; they are terribly united; they think they are contending for their wives, children, and liberty. Their supplies are at hand, ours are three thousand miles off. Are we able to conquer the Americans suppose they are left to themselves? We are not sure of this, nor are we sure that all our neighbors will stand stock still."

Though Bishop Asbury had to keep himself concealed during a part of the Revolutionary period, he was in favor of the independence of the colonies.

At the organization of the denomination in 1784, it was the first religious body of the country to insert in its constitutional law (in its Articles of Religion) a recognition of the new government, enforcing patriotism on its communicants. A very noteworthy modification (peculiarly interesting in our day) was made in this article in the year 1804. In the original article it was affirmed that the "Congress," etc., "are the officers of the United States of America, according to the division of power made to them by the General Act of Confederation," etc., the national constitution having not yet been adopted; but the General Conference of 1804, by a motion of Rev. Ezekiel Cooper, (a man noted for his sagacity,) struck out all allusion to the "Act of Confederation," inserting in its stead "the Constitution of the United States," etc., and declared that "the said states are a *sovereign* and independent *nation*."* Methodism thus deliberately,

* The italics are my own. A recent paper, "The Christian Witness," in the interest of the insurgent South, attacks the Methodist Episcopal Church on account of this amended Article. "We regret," it says, "that we have to mention in this connection what was incorporated into the organization [of the Methodist Episcopal Church] from the beginning, but has been generally overlooked. We refer to the 23d Article of Religion, which is as follows: 'The President, the Congress, the General Assemblies, the Governors, and the Councils of State, as the delegates of the people, are the rulers of the United

and in its constitutional law, recognized that the "Constitution" superseded the "Act of Confederation," and that the republic was no longer a confederacy but a *nation*, and as such, supreme and sovereign over all its states. It was at a period of no little political agitation on the question of state sovereignty that this change was made: the Kentucky "Resolutions of 1798," and those of Virginia, 1799, had become the basis of a State Rights party. A cotemporary Methodist preacher (Henry Boehm, still living) records that just previous to this time "there was great political excitement. Federalism and Democracy ran high—such was the excitement that it separated families, and friends, and members

States of America, according to the division of power made to them by the Constitution of the United States, and by the Constitutions of their respective States. And the said States are a sovereign and independent *nation*, and ought not to be subject to any foreign jurisdiction.'" The "Witness" proceeds to say that "the language of the Article leans very strongly toward an anti-democratic view of the relations between the Federal and the State governments, and has been often so construed by the authorities of the Church since our present political troubles began. It has been referred to again and again by the Annual and General Conferences, by the official papers, and by the bishops and preachers, as decisive of the position which the Church holds upon the subject of State rights." The "Witness" errs in saying this form of the Article existed "from the beginning," but is correct in its statement of the Church's interpretation of the Article. After the adoption of the National Constitution, Methodism never doubted the *sovereign* nationality of the Republic, and never had the unstatesmanlike folly to recognize any State right of secession, or any sovereignty which is not subordinate to the National sovereignty.

of the Church. I was urged, on every side, to identify myself with one political party or the other, or to express an opinion. I felt sad to see what influence this state of feeling was producing in the Church." It was in such circumstances that the Methodist Episcopal Church took its stand for the National Constitution. During the late civil war it has appealed to its Article, as expressing the loyal duty of all its people, and they have responded to the appeal with a patriotic devotion surpassed by no other religious communion of the country.

The Methodist Episcopal Church was also the first religious body to recognize the organization of the national government and the presidency of Washington. Bishops Coke and Asbury, in the name of the Conference in session at New York, waited on Washington, then just inaugurated, on May 29, 1789, and Asbury read to him the address of the Conference. "The address," says a cotemporary preacher, "and the answer, in a few days, were inserted in the public prints; and some of the ministers and members of the other Churches appeared dissatisfied that the Methodists should take the lead. In a few days the other denominations successively followed our example." The Address of the Bishops was signed by Coke and Asbury. It said, "We, the Bishops of the Methodist Episcopal Church, humbly beg leave, in the name of our Society, collectively, in these United States, to express to you the warm feelings of our hearts, and our sincere congratulations on your appointment to the presidentship of these states. We are conscious, from the signal proofs you have already given, that you are a friend of mankind; and under this established idea, place as full confidence in your wisdom and integrity for the preservation of those civil and religious liberties which have been transmitted to us by the providence of God and the glorious Revolution, as we believe ought to be reposed in man. We have received the most grateful satisfaction from the humble and entire dependence on the great Governor of the universe which you have repeatedly expressed, acknowledging him the source of every blessing, and particularly of the most excellent Constitution of these states, which is at present the admiration of the world, and may in future become its great exemplar for imitation; and hence we enjoy a holy expectation, that you will always prove a faithful and impartial patron of genuine vital religion, the grand end of our creation and present probationary existence. And we promise you our fervent prayers to the throne of grace, that God Almighty may endue you with all the graces and gifts of his Holy Spirit, that he may enable you to fill up your important station to his glory, the good of his Church, the happiness and prosperity of the United States, and the welfare of mankind. Signed in behalf of the Methodist Episcopal Church."

Washington, in reply, said: "I return to you individually, and through you to your Society collectively in the United States, my thanks for the demonstrations of affection, and the expressions of joy offered in their behalf, on my late appointment. It shall be my endeavor to manifest the purity of my inclinations for promoting the happiness of mankind, as well of the sincerity of my desires to contribute whatever may be in my power toward the civil and religious liberties of the American people. In pursuing this line of conduct, I hope, by the assistance of Divine Providence, not altogether to disappoint the confidence which you have been pleased to repose in me. It always affords me satisfaction when I find a concurrence of sentiment and practice between all conscientious men, in acknowledgments of homage to the great Governor of the Universe, and in professions of support to a just civil government. After mentioning that I trust the people of every denomination, who demean themselves as good citizens, will have occasion to be convinced that I shall always strive to prove a faithful and impartial patron of genuine vital religion, I must assure you in particular, that I take in the kindest part the promise you make of presenting your prayers at the throne of grace for me, and that I likewise implore the divine benediction on yourselves and your religious community."

These two first bishops of Methodism were intimate with Washington, and were entertained at his table at Mount Vernon, where they held patriotic consultations with him, especially on the subject of slavery, he being, as they have recorded, of their own sentiments on that subject.

On this great national question, which has so fortunately reached its solution in our day, Methodism has always borne a decided testimony, and has contributed more, perhaps, than any other Christian denomination, to its final settlement. If Quakerism has given a less equivocal verdict on the evil, Methodism has done incomparably more effectual work against it. At the organization of the Church it enacted a law against it, and afterward incorporated into its constitutional law (its General Rules or terms of membership) a prohibition of "the buying and selling of men, women, and children, with an intention to enslave them," a law which has kept its honorable record down to this day. The early Methodist preachers, who, like Hatch and Garrettson, inherited, or otherwise came into the possession of slaves, emancipated them. With the rapid spread of the Church southward, its stringent opinions on the subject became lax; violent discussions and parties arose within its communion, and confusion and schism followed; but its primitive standard of opinion at last triumphed, and at the General Conference of 1844, rather than endure further encroachments from the barbarous evil, it suffered the greatest schism in the ecclesiastical history of the country, the secession of the Methodist Episcopal Church South, by which it lost at a stroke nearly half its members and half its territory.

In the further progress of the antislavery controversy as a national question, no religious communion of the country has been more energetic than Methodism. It was the first denomination to enter practically and prominently into the contest, notwithstanding the opposition of many of its strongest men; and if, in its southern and schismatic people, have been found the strongest abettors of slavery and rebellion, northern Methodism has redeemed the denominational honor by its uncompromising devotion to the slave and the Constitution. A Methodist conference (the New York East Conference) was the first ecclesiastical body to pledge its loyal and utter co-operation with the government, after the attack on Fort Sumter; and by a happy coincidence was the first to telegraph congratulations to the government at the downfall of the rebellion, by the surrender of Lee.* Methodism has contributed, it

* This Conference happened to be holding sessions at the time of each of these events.

has been estimated, a hundred thousand white and seventy-five thousand black troops to the war for the Union. The Methodist Episcopal Church has thinned its congregations, disbanded many of its Sunday-school and Bible classes, by these patriotic contributions. Its pulpits have resounded through the war with enthusiastic pleas for the Constitution. Its entire denominational press (the most extensive in the land) has, without one exception, been fervently and continually devoted to the national cause. The national flag has waved from its spires and draped its pulpits, and its characteristic enthusiasm has been kindled to the highest fervor by the national struggle. Many of its preachers have followed the army as chaplains, others as officers, and others as privates. Thousands of Methodist martyrs for the Union sleep under the sod of southern battle-fields. In fine, Methodism, as the chief religious embodiment of the common people, has felt that its destiny is identical with that of the country, and has thrown its utmost energy into the great struggle for the national life. The government has recognized its services, and, at its last General Conference, President Lincoln addressed it an emphatic testimonial, saying: "Nobly sustained as the Government has been by all the Churches, I would utter nothing which might in the least appear invidious against any. Yet without this it may fairly be said that the Methodist

Episcopal Church, not less devoted than the best, is, by its greater numbers, the most important of all. It is no fault in others that the Methodist Church sends more soldiers to the field, more nurses to the hospitals, and more prayers to heaven than any. God bless the Methodist Church! bless all the Churches! and blessed be God! who in this our great trial giveth us the Churches."

CHAPTER VII.

SUMMARY VIEW.

SUCH, then, is Methodism, historically viewed; such the results which entitle its birth in the New World to the grateful commemoration of its people.

Embury's little congregation of five persons, in his own house, has multiplied to thousands of Societies, from the northernmost settlements of Canada to the Gulf of Mexico, from Nova Scotia to California. The first small conference of 1773, with its 10 preachers and its 1,160 reported members, has multiplied to 60 conferences, 6,821 itinerant, 8,205 local preachers, and 928,320 members in the Methodist Episcopal Church alone, exclusive of the southern, the Canadian and minor branches, all the offspring of the Church founded in 1766 and episcopally organized in 1784.

It has property in churches and parsonages amounting to about $27,000,000.

It has 25 colleges and theological schools, with property amounting to $3,055,000, 158 instructors, and 5,345 students; and 77 academies, with 556 instructors and 17,761 students; making a body of 714 instructors, and an army of 23,106 students.

Its church property, (churches, parsonages, and colleges, aside from its 77 academies and Book Concern,) amounts to $30,055,000.

Its Book Concern has a capital of $837,000; 500 publishing agents, editors, clerks, and operatives; with some thirty cylinder power presses in constant operation, about 2,000 different books on its catalogue, besides tracts, etc.; 14 periodicals, with an aggregate circulation of more than 1,000,000 copies per month.*

Its Sunday-School Union comprises 13,400 schools; more than 150,000 instructors; nearly 918,000 pupils; and more than 2,500,000 library books. It issues nearly 2,500 publications, besides a monthly circulation of nearly 300,000 numbers of its periodicals.

Its Missionary Society has 1,059 circuits and stations; 1,128 paid laborers, and 105,675 communicants.

The Methodist Episcopal Church South has published no statistics since the rebellion broke out; it has doubtless suffered much by the war, but it reported, the last year before the rebellion, nearly 700,000 Church members, nearly 2,600 itinerant and 5,000 local members. It had 12 periodical publications, 12 colleges, and 77 academies, with 8,000 stu-

* There are five independent weekly papers in the Church besides the above number of "official" periodicals.

dents. Its Missionary Society sustained, at home and abroad, about 360 missionaries and 8 manual labor schools, with nearly 500 pupils.

According to these figures the two great Episcopal divisions of the denomination have had, at their latest reports, 1,628,320 members; 9,421 traveling, and 13,205 local preachers; with 191 colleges and academies, and 31,106 students.*

The Canada Wesleyan Church was not only founded by, but for many years belonged to, the Methodist Episcopal Church; it now reports more than 56,000 members, 500 itinerant preachers, and 750 Sunday-schools with about 45,000 pupils; a university, a female college, and a Book Concern with its weekly periodical.

Another branch of Canadian Methodism, the "Methodist Episcopal Church in Canada," equally the child of the Methodist Episcopal Church in the United States, reports 3 Annual Conferences, 2 bishops, 216 traveling and 224 local preachers, and 20,000 members; a seminary and female college, and a weekly newspaper.

The Canadian Wesleyan Methodist New Connec-

* Some of these figures differ slightly from enumerations given elsewhere in this volume; the latter were made from earlier data, and went to press before the former reached me; they do not, however, materially affect the aggregates. Methodism, in common with other Churches, has suffered by the late period of political and military agitation.

tion Church reports 90 traveling and 147 local preachers, and 8,450 communicants. It sustains a weekly paper and a theological school.

The other Methodist bodies, in the United States, are the Methodist Protestant Church, the American Wesleyan Methodists, the African Methodist Episcopal Church, and some three or four smaller sects; their aggregate membership amounts to about 260,000; their preachers to 3,423.*

Adding the traveling preachers to the membership, there are now in the United States about 1,901,164 Methodist communicants. Adding three non-communicant members of its congregations for each communicant, it has under its influence 7,604,656 souls—between one fifth and one fourth of the whole national population.

Aggregately there are now in the United States and Canada,† as the results of the Methodism of 1766, 1,972,770 Church members, 13,650 traveling preachers, 15,000 local preachers, nearly 200 colleges and academies, and more than 30 periodical publications; 1,986,420 communicants, including preachers, and nearly 8,000,000 people.

The influence of this vast ecclesiastical force on

* As reported in 1860, in Schem's Ecclesiastical Year Book; our best authority in American ecclesiastical statistics.

† The other North American British Provinces are not included, as their Methodism did not originate with the denomination in the United States. The Primitive Methodists are also omitted.

the moral, intellectual, and social progress of the New World, can neither be doubted nor measured. It is generally conceded that it has been the most energetic religious element in the social development cf the continent. With its devoted and enterprising people dispersed through the whole population, its thousands of laborious itinerant preachers, and tens of thousands of local preachers and exhorters, its unequaled publishing agencies and powerful periodicals, from the Quarterly Review to the child's paper, its hundreds of colleges and academies, its hundreds of thousands of Sunday-school instructors, its devotion to the lower and most needy classes, its animated modes of worship and religious labor, it cannot be questioned that it has been a mighty, if not the mightiest agent in the maintenance and spread of Protestant Christianity over these lands. It stands now on the threshold of its second century mightier than ever, in all the elements and resources requisite for a still greater history. It has modified somewhat its primitive methods, but only for its increased efficiency.

The question, What is the actual position, moral as well as statistical, of the Methodist Episcopal Church in particular? cannot be more authoritatively answered than in the address of its latest delegate to the British Conference, Bishop Janes. "In this epoch of her history," he says, "the question naturally arises, 'What has been the career of American Methodism, what its attainments of power and usefulness in the land and in the world?' As a partial answer to this inquiry, we refer you to our latest tables of statistics:* Communicants, 928,320; itinerant ministers, 6,821; local ministers, 8,205; churches, 10,015; parsonages, 2,948; estimated value of churches and parsonages, $26,883,076; Sunday-schools, 13,153; officers and teachers, 148,475; scholars, 859,700. We have 161 missionaries in foreign lands, and 7,022 church members. Among the foreign populations of our own country, we have laboring 286 missionaries; and in the churches under their care, 26,138 communicants. In our domestic missionary department we have about 800 missionaries; their statistics are given in the general aggregate I have stated. Some of these missionaries are supported wholly by the missionary fund, but most of them only in part. Receipts, $558,993; the appropriations for the current year are $625,000. With regard to our education, we have 23 universities or colleges, in which there are 5,345 students, with property and endowment funds amounting to more than $2,800,000. We have two theological schools, in which there are 116

* The statistics, given elsewhere in this volume, are the latest I have been able to obtain; a difference of time will account for any difference of figures between the bishop's statements and my own.

students, with property valued at $150,000.* We have 77 academic institutions, with about 18,000 students, the number of males and females being about equal. Our use of the press has been continually increasing. We have now nine weekly and several semi-monthly, monthly, and quarterly periodicals, which are official, and several unofficial periodicals which are Methodistic in their character. We still follow the example of Mr. Wesley in zealously circulating Christian books. We have a very large number of Sunday-school publications, and a religious literature adapted to the wants of the whole Church. These statistics only answer the question partially. There have been several large secessions from the Church, which have continued to preach our doctrines and observe most of our usages. I have not been permitted to examine the 'Book of Life' to ascertain the great number who shared her militant fellowship on earth, but now enjoy the divine fruition of the Church triumphant in heaven. Could I obtain the number of those, living and dead, who have been enrolled in the annals of American Methodism, even that would not give the full measure of its usefulness. Its influence, subtle as the fragrance of the flower, could not be registered by man. 'As the dew of Hermon, and the dew that descended upon the mountain when

* This does not include the legacy of the late Mrs. Garrett.

the Lord commanded the blessing,' the influence of American Methodism has descended upon the whole land, permeating more or less all denominations of Christians, and germinating and maturing many rich fruits, which have been garnered in other Churches and recorded in other registers. It is, perhaps, a most important question for us to answer whether the American Methodism of 1865 is the Methodism introduced in 1766. Notwithstanding all that croakers and grumblers have said or can say on this subject, a careful examination will show that if it does not strictly retain the resemblance of the impression to the signet, it does bear the identity of manhood to childhood, of the harvest to the seed. Changes have been made in the 'Rules and Regulations' from time to time, by legitimate authority, as the exigencies of the Church have required. It is exceedingly interesting to see how these changes have been made in the direction of development, of enlargement, and of progress.

"The Methodist Episcopal Church was organized by authority of Mr. Wesley, in 1784, by Dr. Coke. The liturgy which Mr. Wesley provided for the Church contained the forms of making and ordaining superintendents or bishops, and elders or presbyters, and deacons. The discipline he gave the Church provided for employment of unordained ministers and local preachers to assist the pastors in their pulpit labors, and class-leaders to aid them in their pastoral work. These are the orders and duties of our ministers and pastors at this present time. The number of ministers soon became so large, and their distance from each other so great, that it was found impossible for them to meet in one conference. Two conferences were then formed. As these became inconveniently large, they were again divided; and this process has been continued, until now, including our conferences in Africa and Germany, and India, we have sixty Annual Conferences. For the same reason, it was found necessary to provide for a delegated General Conference, to meet quadrennially, with authority, under certain specified restrictions, 'to make rules and regulations' for the Church, to review the administration of the Annual Conference, and to elect and ordain bishops whenever the state of the work required it. We have also a Quarterly Conference, composed of the preachers of the circuit, the local preachers, stewards, trustees, class-leaders, exhorters, and Sunday-school superintendents. This conference has a general but prescribed supervision of all the interests of the circuit. The few simple rules which Mr. Wesley provided for removing improper persons from society and improper ministers from the conference have been elaborated into a complete system of ecclesiastical jurisprudence. We maintain, unimpaired, the itinerancy of our ministry. In the older and more densely populated portions of the country, the work is divided into stations or separate pastoral charges. In the newer and more sparsely peopled sections we retain the circuit form. The late General Conference extended the term of ministerial service so as to allow a minister to remain three years in the same charge. The Episcopacy constitutes an 'Itinerant General Superintendency.' There is no feature of our polity of which both the ministers and laity of the Church are more jealous. The attachment to it is universal. Attendance upon class-meeting has not been uniformly enforced as a condition of Church membership. The duty of attendance upon this social means of grace has been strongly urged upon all our members. Many of the pastors have laid aside for a breach of our rules such members as were delinquents in this respect. The institution is very highly appreciated by the spiritual and devout portion of the Church. It is invaluable in training our converts. Our leaders, taken as a body, make a sub-pastorate, a lay agency which is unequaled. The local preachers and class-leaders of the Methodist Episcopal Church constitute one of the grand forces of American Methodism.

"Does the Methodist Episcopal Church retain its simplicity and spirituality? Is it being built up with living stones? Is it a spiritual house, a holy priesthood, offering up spiritual sacrifices acceptable to God through Jesus Christ. We cannot search the hearts or discern the spirits of our brethren. We can only judge from outward signs, and even thus with great carefulness. Most of our members bring forth the fruits of good living. They testify in class-meetings and love-feasts, and on other suitable occasions, to their enjoyment of God's pardoning mercy and adopting love, many of them of his sanctifying power. Our people almost uniformly prefer spiritual scriptural preaching. We are favored with frequent and extensive revivals; and we can and do feel and say, 'the best of all is, God is with us.' As to the future, our success is likely to be greater than ever."

PART III.

ITS CAPABILITIES AND RESPONSIBILITIES FOR THE FUTURE.

THE capabilities of American Methodism, for continued and increased usefulness, have already been shown in the historical view of its practical methods, its theological teachings, and its actual results. It stands strong to-day in its essential doctrines and methods; and it has the additional ability and responsibility of greater financial resources than it has ever had before. Its people, originally the poorest of the land, have become, under its beneficent training, perhaps the wealthiest. Not only has it more diffused wealth than any sister denomination, but its cases of individual opulence have, within the last quarter of a century, greatly multiplied. As the leading Church of the country, it bears, before God and man, the chief responsibility of the moral welfare of the nation. *The better consecration of its wealth to the public good is therefore one of the principal responsibilities of its future.*

We have seen how providentially it met the moral exigencies which grew out of the early rapid growth of the American population; exigencies that could not otherwise have been met. But a greater demand, if possible, is to be made upon it in the future. This wonderful growth of population—is to advance at a rate which threatens to outstrip the provisions for its intellectual and religious training. In less than forty years from the present date more than one hundred millions of human souls will be dependent upon these provisions for their intellectual and moral nutriment. They bear now no adequate relation to the real necessities of the land. If, after more than two centuries of religious and educational efforts, under the most auspicious circumstances of the country, we have but partially provided for thirty-five millions, how shall we, in forty years, meet the immensely enlarged moral wants of nearly three times that number? The question is a very grave one. Our rapid growth, so much the boast of the nation, is not without imminent peril; it may be too rapid to be healthful; it is to be the severest test of both our religion and our liberties, for one is the essential condition of the other. And yet it cannot, by any probable contingencies, be restrained. It has a momentum which will bear down and overleap all the ordinary obstructions of population. We cannot want work, we cannot want bread; and where these exist, population must advance as inevitably as the waters under the laws of the tide. Every growth of this population provides indeed somewhat, morally as well as materially, for the next growth; but the law of proportion must fail in this respect, under our rapid advance and the peculiar elements of our growth, unless the religious bodies of the land, to which its education is so largely confided, make special provisions for it.

When we remind ourselves that so much of this popular increase is from abroad, that Europe has been in an "exodus" toward our shores, that its ignorance and vice—wave overtopping wave—roll in upon the land, the danger assumes a startling aspect. In about thirty-six years from this day our population will equal the present aggregate population of England, France, Switzerland, Spain, Portugal, Sweden, and Denmark. A step further in the calculation presents a prospect still more surprising and impressive: in about sixty-six years from to-day this mighty mass of commingled peoples will have swollen to the stupendous aggregate of two hundred and forty-six millions—equaling the present population of all Europe. According to the statistics of life, there are hundreds of thousands of our present population who will witness this truly grand result. What have the friends of education and religion to do within that time! If our present intellectual and moral provisions for the people are far short of the wants of our present thirty-five millions, how in sixty-six years shall we provide for more than two hundred and eleven additional millions, and these millions, to a great extent, composed of semi-barbarous foreigners and their mistrained children?

We may well ponder these facts, and feel that on us, the citizens of the republic, at this the middle of the nineteenth century, devolves a moral exigency such as, perhaps, no other land ever saw; an exigency as full of sublimity as of urgency—as grand in its opportunity as in its peril. This immense prospective population—certain, though prospective—is to be thrown out, by the almighty hand of Providence, upon one of the grandest arenas of the world. Here, on this large continent, bounded in its distant independence by the Atlantic, the Pacific, the great tropic gulf, and the Arctic; here, away from the traditional governments and faiths and other antiquated checks of the old world, it is to play its great drama of destiny—a destiny which, as we have shown, must, numerically at least, be in less than seventy years as potential as all present Europe, and how much more potential in all moral, political, and commercial respects? What an idea would it be, that of all Europe consolidated into one mighty, untrammeled commonwealth, in the highest liberty, religious enlighten-nent, and industrial development—and this mighty revolution to be completed in less than seventy years from to-day? Who would credit the conception? Yet our republic will, in that time, more than realize the stupendous idea, if its political and moral integrity be not sacrificed.

Look at its field. According to an official report, the total area of the United States and territories in 1853 was 2,983,153 square miles. This estimate is found to be even short of the truth: various official reports from the Land Office, and the aggregate of the census, show 3,220,572 square miles. It is estimated from these facts that the territorial extent of the republic is nearly ten times as large as that of Great Britain and France united, three times as large as the whole of Britain, France, Austria, Prussia, Spain, Portugal, Belgium, Holland, and Denmark; one and a half times as large as the Russian empire in Europe; only a sixth less than the area covered by the nearly sixty empires, states, or republics of Europe; of larger extent than the Roman empire, or that of Alexander, neither of which exceeded three millions of square miles. What a theater is this for the achievements of civilization and religion! Surely there should be "giants in these days" to enact worthily the enterprises of such a field. And if circumstances make men, are we not to hope that the consciousness of this unparalleled destiny will enlarge and ennoble the intellect, the philanthropy, and moral energy of the country to a scale of corresponding magnificence—will bring forth sublime examples of public devotion, of talent, of moral heroism, and of munificence? Let it be repeated that Methodism, by its numerical strength and wealth, has a larger responsibility for this great field than any other Church of the land.

American Methodism, as we have seen, has been remarkable for the progress of its *Educational provisions;* and this fact may be considered one of its providential adaptations to its great mission in the New World. Wisely has its General Conference "Centenary Committee" proposed to commemorate its centenary jubilee, not so much by a monumental *edifice* as by a monumental *institution*—a permanent fund for education. An impressive argument for education is found in the large proportion of our juvenile population. Where there is plenty of food, as there must indefinitely be in this country, there will always be plenty of children. It is a beneficent, a beautiful law. Nearly half our present white population are yet in what may be called the flower of youth. We almost literally present an example of national adolescence—the freshness, the ardor, the vigor, and the susceptibility of childhood and young manhood.

Our white population in 1860 was 26,957,471; the portion which was under twenty years of age, 12,614,637. The destiny of the country is then in the hands of its educators. The population of to-day is to surpass all the millions of Europe in less than seventy years; and its educators hold within their power nearly one half of the population of to-day, nearly one half the present elements of the grand geometrical progression. Let them work out, then, with an untiring hand and a sublime consciousness, this mighty arithmetic of destiny! It may be soberly said that never before was there a battle-field for humanity like this; never were the elements of good and evil set forth against each other in a grander arena; never was humanity thrown out upon conditions more experimental, more free from the trammels of old institutions, of old traditions, of old fallacies. It must be mighty here—that is inevitable; but it will be mighty in the strength of its wickedness, like the antediluvian giants who brought the world to dissolution, or mighty in the virtues which shall subdue the world to the reign of religion, intelligence, and liberty. They who have the means of educating the young can lay a mightier hand upon this sublime future than any other heroes in the field. The legislators of the land, its high places of power, and of professional life, may do much for it; but its humble places of education, including its Sunday-schools, are its true fortresses—"the cheap defense of the nation."

It is to be hoped, therefore, that Methodism, with its chief responsibility for the moral and intellectual progress of the country, will prosecute more vigorously than ever its educational work, and that it will especially crown its present jubilee by endowing, in accordance with the plan of its Centenary Committee, a monumental fund for education, which shall worthily commemorate the great occasion, and from which not only its present numerous colleges shall receive additional strength, but new ones shall spring up as the population of the country advances.

It should especially enlarge its means of ministerial education. It has done a great work in the mere conquest (now universal) of the popular prejudice against theological schools. It has provided, as we have seen, two such institutions, one in the north-east and one in the north-west; it needs at least three more immediately: one in the middle East, one in the middle West, and one on the Pacific coast. It should have them, at latest, within five years, and its proposed Centenary fund will probably enable it to provide them even earlier.* Ministerial

* Daniel Drew, Esq., has already pledged $250,000 for a theological school near New York City, the first centenary donation to the Church, and one worthy of the occasion.

education is evidently one of its greatest necessities for the future; it is not only necessary for its progress, but for the safety of the great conquests it has already won. Its people are rapidly advancing in intelligence; their demand for improved pulpit instruction cannot be waived; it must be met, or their families be lost from the denomination. The Church has become conscious of this necessity, and will not, it is to be hoped, delay to provide abundantly for it.

Methodism should feel itself responsible to minister hereafter, more than heretofore, to the public culture, by the improvement of its church architecture. During most of its history, it has had to extemporize its temples. Within the last twenty-five years it has been providentially enabled to renew a large proportion of them, to give them better locations, better internal accommodations, and better architectural style; so that in some of the principal cities, Boston, New York, Newark, Philadelphia, Wilmington, Chicago, Cincinnati, its places of worship are rapidly taking rank with those of older denominations. It has need, indeed, of caution against excess in this respect, but it has more need of liberal taste than of caution, for its error has been in the opposite direction, if not in the opposite extreme. It should bear in mind that its permanent hold upon its congregations, especially in the larger communities, will depend much upon the convenience and even the elegance (the just elegance) of its churches; that there can be no moral objection to good taste and genuine art; and that the monuments of religion deserve such tributes above all other structures. The taste of the Church has advanced much in this respect, more, perhaps, than its liberality, but it needs further training in both. It needs to be reminded that true taste and true art are not adventitious things, much less the products of pride or luxury; that they are founded in original laws, that is to say, divine laws of human nature, and therefore meet a natural want of man; that even the strictest "utilitarianism" cannot rationally condemn them, for beauty is often the highest utility, ministering, in art, to our higher wants in a manner incomparably more utilitarian, than the service of the lower or "practical arts" to our lower nature. God has written its vindication over all his works, for whatever may be their mechanical processes and directly utilitarian designs, he has decorated them everywhere with beauty or sublimity, and their very first appeal is to our minds rather than to our physical necessities. The heavens by day and by night, the mountains and valleys, the streams and seas, and most living things, are made by him pictures for the soul before they can be made by us tributary to our material wants. He permits not the vegetable world to yield us bread, till it has first yielded beauty through the eye, to the mind. The blossom precedes the fruit. True art should be recognized as one of the noblest handmaids of religion; elevating impressions and associations, through the senses in our temples, may ennoble even divine worship; and imposing monuments of taste, consecrated to piety, are among the highest means of national culture, and the highest proofs of advanced civilization. It is a sacred peculiarity of architectural art that, unlike painting and sculpture, it will not lend itself to vice; its severe and stately beauty disdains effeminate or voluptuous tastes. It is the most sublime, the most religious, of the works of man.

On really utilitarian grounds, then, may we plead for religious art. Yet we may plead for it also on really economical grounds. The most expensive temple is usually the most economical. The Church that builds its edifice in the most eligible locality and in the most attractive style, almost invariably finds its expense the best reimbursed, by its command of the people, their attendance, their intelligence, and their money. A well located, substantial, and commanding temple aids much in giving security to a Church, and is cheap in this respect. The stability of the religions of the old world, their power over local populations, are owing largely to their grand edifices. Methodism should not despise this power. It must still throw up hastily, especially in its frontier fields, temporary "meeting-houses," shanties, or log-cabins; it should multiply greatly its cheap suburban temples; but it should make all prudent haste to supersede these by better structures. Consulting always, and primarily, practical convenience in its buildings, it should also endeavor liberally to ennoble the house of God by every aid of genuine taste and art. It will not be able to justify itself against the claims of public opinion and public taste upon it if, with its great prosperity, it should fail to have within the next twenty-five years the most approved and most commodious churches of the nation.

It should be one of its most earnest aims to consolidate its forces by the union of its various American branches. There would seem to be but temporary, if indeed any reason, for the continued separation of its two chief bodies, north and south. They divided on the question of slavery; that question is now practically obsolete; they are identical in their theological and practical systems and in their ecclesiastical aims; their reunion would contribute much to the social and political reconciliation of the North and South; it is a duty, therefore, that they both owe to their common country, and to our common

Christianity. On what terms such a reconciliation should be founded, need not here be discussed; it is sufficient to affirm the obvious fact that it should be effected, and whatever is obviously right is always, sooner or later, practicable. The other branches of American Methodism have arisen mostly by secessions, founded on questions of church government, especially on the demand for lay representation. The position of the supreme assembly of the Church on this subject, its readiness at the will of the Church to make the change, should make it possible for such sister bodies to return to the common household.

Such a consolidation of the various communions which bear the name of Methodists and have identical doctrines and discipline, would mightily strengthen, numerically and morally, the common cause. Perhaps a still greater advantage would be the diminution of the prevalent sectarianism of the country, and the consequent abatement of its rancor, its wastefulness, and its bad moral effect on the public mind. Whatever may be the advantage of a variety of religious denominations, for the accommodation of a variety of religious opinions or scruples, (an advantage enormously exaggerated in this country,) it surely cannot justify those distinctions, without an essential difference, which the various sects of Methodism now present. If American Christianity must needs have divisions, it certainly need not have these subdivisions. Wesley gloried, as we have seen, in the liberality, the catholicity of Methodism; it is a boast which his disciples should be eager to maintain throughout the world and to the end of time. What a crowning glory would it be to its centenary jubilee, if all its now practically unnecessary branches could be blended into one common cause before the joyous year (never to be enjoyed on earth by any of us again) has passed away! If this be impossible, can we not, at least, in the proceedings of this memorable year, lay with certainty the foundations of so grand a consummation?

Methodism should earnestly seek to solve that now most important of its practical problems, how to secure its children within its own pale. Its Sunday-schools help it much in this respect, but not sufficiently. Thousands of its youth have been annually converted within these schools: nearly 19,000 the last year, (1864,) nearly 40,000 within the last two years; more than 285,000 within the last eighteen years. In several of these years the reported conversions in the schools equaled half the annual additions to the Church membership; in several the former more than equaled the whole of the latter. In the entire period the Sunday-school conversions have surpassed the entire gains of the Church membership by nearly 5,000. During three years of the war the membership decreased 67,000, but during these same three years the reported conversions in the schools amounted to 50,500. While these facts speak emphatically for the religious power of the school, they show alarmingly the inefficient guardianship of the Church over its children. They prove that most of its converted youth either fail to enter or are lost from its communion. The startling exhibit of these statistics should be kept under the eye of the Church,* and be anxiously pondered till a remedy be found for the extraordinary evil. The last General Conference ordained that the "baptized children of the Church" shall be "organized into classes," with suitable leaders, (male or female,) and in due time be "enrolled on the list of probationers" and "admitted into full membership." This is an important advance in the right direction; but it must fail without the diligent pastoral attention of the ministry. The intimate co-operation of the pastor with his Sunday-school teachers; his presence in the school, especially in

* Year.	Total conversions.	Increase of Ch. Membership.	Year.	Total conversions.	Increase of Ch. Membership.
1847	4,118	Dec.	1857	14,669	20,192
1848	8,240	7,508	1858	32,315	136,036
1849	9,014	23,249	1859	20,580	17,790
1850	11,398	27,367	1860	19,517	20,102
1851	14,557	32,122	1861	17,498	dec. 1,924
1852	13,243	6,896	1862	12,828	dec. 45,617
1853	16,916	3,937	1863	20,233	dec. 19,512
1854	17,494	30,732	1864	18,892	4,926
1855	17,443	16,073			
1856	16,775	896		285,730	280,773

times of religious interest; his habitual personal care of converted scholars until they shall be fully incorporated and confirmed in the Church, and his continual endeavors to interest them in their religious duties, are indispensable means of their safety. He should behold in the Sunday-school the Church of the future. There more than anywhere else should we exert our utmost strength, for thence chiefly are we to reinforce our hosts for all coming battles and victories. The great number of reported conversions in our schools, probably exceeding that of any other, if not indeed of all other American Churches combined, should thrill the denomination with interest, should convince it that here it has a field of immeasurable resources, and that I have not wrongly called the question of the Church relation of its children its greatest practical problem.

Finally, and above all things, Methodism should be reminded of its responsibility to maintain vital, apostolic piety in the land, and to spread it over the world. This, as we have seen, was its original mission; this its historical stand-point; from this has sprung all its surprising achievements; if this ceases the light will go out in all its sanctuaries. Its spiritual life has, let it be repeated, preserved its doctrinal integrity and its practical vigor through these hundred years. It has never had, at least in

America, a serious outbreak of theological heresy. Seldom has it had even an individual judicial case of heterodoxy. Such causes of faction and division have been almost unknown to it. Its piety has kept it orthodox, notwithstanding the extraordinary liberality of its terms of membership. Doubtless its peculiar methods have been the proximate cause of its great success, but what would these methods have been without the spiritual energy which has worked them? That energy has been divine, but the energy of the Divine Spirit itself works by the truth; the doctrines of Methodism have therefore been its vital element. Repentance, faith, personal regeneration, the witness of the Spirit, sanctification, these have been the living ideas of Methodist teaching through out the world. It retains these vital truths to-day unimpaired; let it continue to guard them sacredly, as the very fire on its altars. Let it incessantly expound and enforce them in all its sanctuaries, and these sanctuaries shall continue to be thronged with inquiring, awakened, and living souls.

Reviewing thus with grateful joy the blessings of God to us and our families through his Church, and reminding ourselves, with devout self-admonition, of our responsibility for the future, it is befitting that we should erect, not in stone, but in more enduring substance, a monument, the light on whose summit shall shine with ever increasing glory during the coming hundred years, and shall be witnessed by the eyes of our posterity, when on the anniversary morning of October, 1966, they shall throng in redoubled hosts to their temples, and respond back over our graves, to this anniversary epoch, and send forward to the next the anthems of our jubilee. God grant that the hymns of that morning may resound not only over this, but over both American continents, from Labrador to Terra del Fuego, and that the missions of Methodism may respond to them from all the ends of the earth! Our chief memorial of the epoch, as has been stated, is not to be a building but an institution—a Fund for Education;* the interest of which alone is to be expended, the principal to be handed down as our salutation to the Methodists who shall assemble on that far-off morning. A more practicable or more sublime design is hardly possible to the denomination. Its other leading interests, like missions, Sunday-schools, etc., have the habitual sympathy and support of its people, but education can hardly expect such support, and yet can it be pronounced a less important, though it may be a less direct interest of the Church? Were its centenary contributions to be given to these more immediate interests, they would soon be absorbed or expended,

* The Centenary plan, as appended to this volume, provides for special contributions for other objects, including a Centenary Missionary building; but these are comparatively minor designs.

profitably indeed, but in such manner as to lose their monumental character. The Church can confide these interests to its current sympathy and help, but education needs permanent endowment, and a great educational fund, like that proposed, is of all Church interests the best fitted to be monumental. It can continually assist our existing seminaries and erect new ones, and yet its undiminished principal be transmitted as our benediction to the future. Let us then establish it on a scale worthy not only of the last, but of the next hundred years of our history.

With such a history, such capabilities, and such responsibilities and aims, we enter upon the hundredth year of our great mission. The eye of Christendom will be specially upon us this year. The eye of God will be specially upon us. All the doings of the year should be done as in the sight of him and of his whole catholic Church. At the close of the memorable year, both he and his general Church will judge us according to our works. We shall then also be compelled to judge ourselves. The measure of our gratitude for such great prosperity, of our sense of such great responsibility, and of our Christian zeal for the improvement of such a sublime opportunity, will be apparent to ourselves and to all the world. Surely we shall not, we cannot, fail to rise to the high occasion. We will consecrate it with hymns of acclamation, with prayer, with the renewal of our religious vows, and unequaled offerings of treasure. The first donation for the occasion has already been tendered, and has never been equaled by any personal act of liberality in the history of Methodism. If it cannot be equaled by other donors, yet should it be a standard by which we should all proportionately measure our liberality. Should a dollar be laid on the altar of the Church this year by each of its recorded members, the sum will be nearly a million. There is scarcely one of them, young or old, who cannot give this pittance. It should be the resolution of the Church that every member shall thus have a share in its offerings; every Society in the connection should see that it be obtained, and should provide it for any individual case of extreme poverty, if any such there be, where it cannot be afforded. Besides this amount of nearly a million, we can expect thousands of gifts from five dollars to five, ten, or twenty thousand each, and probably some of still greater amount. Thus while in acts of worship around our altars we celebrate the centenary festival, let us heap upon those altars the palpable proofs of the sincerity of our gratitude, and by the close of the joyous year, present to the Christian world an example of beneficence which shall never be forgotten.

CONNECTIONAL ARRANGEMENTS

FOR THE CELEBRATION OF THE

CENTENARY OF AMERICAN METHODISM,

1866,

AS AUTHORIZED BY THE GENERAL CONFERENCE, AND THE COMMITTEES APPOINTED BY ITS ORDER.

BY JOHN M'CLINTOCK, D.D.

CONNECTIONAL PLAN

FOR THE CELEBRATION OF THE

CENTENARY OF AMERICAN METHODISM.

ORDER OF THE GENERAL CONFERENCE.

THE General Conference of the Methodist Episcopal Church, at its session in Philadelphia, 1864, adopted the following preamble and resolutions:

Whereas, Methodism in the United States of America will complete the first century of its history in 1866;

And *whereas*, under the special blessing of God, it has risen in power and extended in usefulness to a degree hardly paralleled in the history of the Church;

And especially in view of the many thousands that have been saved through its instrumentality, the influence it has exerted upon the theology of its times and the evangelization of the world, we deem it right to observe the closing period of this first centenary with special solemnities and pious offerings, which shall present before God some humble expression of our devout gratitude, and lead to a renewed consecration of ourselves, our services and means to the glory of our Divine Master; therefore be it

Resolved, By the delegates of the Annual Conferences of the Methodist Episcopal Church in General Conference assembled, as follows:

1. The centenary of Methodism in America shall be cele-

brated by all our Churches and people with devout thanksgiving, by special religious services and liberal thank-offerings.

2. This celebration shall commence on the first Tuesday in October, 1866, and continue through the month, at such times and places as may best suit the convenience of the Societies.

3. The primary object of the celebration shall be the spiritual improvement of our members, and especially by reviewing the great things God hath wrought for us, the cultivating of feelings of gratitude for the blessings received through the agency of Methodism.

4. As the gratitude of the heart ever seeks expression in outward acts, we invite as a spontaneous offering to Almighty God on this occasion pecuniary contributions from each "according as God hath prospered him," to be so appropriated as to render more efficient in the century to come those institutions and agencies to which the Church has been so deeply indebted in the century past.

5. Two departments of Christian enterprise shall be placed before our people, one connectional, central, and monumental, the other local and distributive, and all shall be urged to make liberal appropriations to both according to their own discretion.

6. The Board of Bishops shall appoint twelve traveling preachers and twelve laymen, who, in connection with the members of their own Board, shall be a committee to determine to what objects and in what proportions the moneys raised as connectional funds shall be appropriated, and have power to take all steps necessary to their proper distribution.

7. The local funds shall be appropriated to the cause of education and church extension under the direction of a committee consisting of an equal number of ministers and laymen appointed by the several Annual Conferences within the bounds of which they are raised.

8. Each Annual Conference shall provide for the delivery of a memorial sermon before its own body at the session next preceding the centennial celebration, and also appoint a committee of an equal number of ministers and laymen to give advice and direction for the appropriate celebration of the centennial in our principal Churches.

9. As the highest authority of the Methodist Episcopal Church, we commend this whole subject to the prayerful consideration of every minister, traveling and local, and every official and private member of the Church, calling for the most systematic and energetic efforts everywhere to carry out in their true spirit these noble plans; and after due consideration, we deem it right to ask for and to expect not less than two millions of dollars for achievements which will be worthy of our great and honored Church, and which shall show to our descendants to the latest generations the gratitude we feel for the wonderful Providence which originated and has so largely blessed and prospered our beloved Church.

10. We cordially invite our brethren in all the branches of the great Methodist family, in this and in other lands, to unite with us in this grand Centennial Celebration, that together we may lift our thanksgivings to the God of our fathers, and renew our consecration to his spiritual service.—*Journal of General Conference*, 1864, pp. 445–447.

COMMITTEE APPOINTED BY THE BISHOPS.

In accordance with the sixth of the above resolutions, the Board of Bishops appointed the following persons, to constitute, together with the Bishops, the Committee:

Ministers.

Rev. George Peck, D.D.; Rev. Charles Elliott, D.D.; Rev. John M'Clintock, D.D.; Rev. D. P. Kidder, D.D.; Rev. D. Patten, D.D.; Rev. E. Thomas; Rev. D. W. Bartine, D.D.; Rev. F. C. Holliday, D.D; Rev. Thomas Sewall, D.D.; Rev. James F. Chalfant; Rev. Moses Hill; Rev. F. A. Blades.

Laymen.

Thomas T. Tasker, Esq., Philadelphia; George C. Cook, Esq., Chicago, Illinois; The Hon. James Bishop, New Brunswick, New Jersey; John Owen, Esq., Detroit, Michigan; Isaac Rich, Esq., Boston; General Clinton B. Fisk, St. Louis, Missouri; I. P. Cook, Esq., Baltimore, Maryland; The Hon. Cary A. Trimble, Chillicothe, Ohio; Oliver Hoyt, Esq., New York city; Alexander Bradley, Esq., Pittsburgh, Pennsylvania; F. H. Root, Esq., Buffalo, New York; Edward Sargent, Esq., Cincinnati, Ohio.

This committee was convened, by the Board of Bishops, at Cleveland, Ohio, February 22, 1865.

ACTION OF THE GENERAL COMMITTEE.

At the time appointed, the committee met at Cleveland. All the bishops were present except Bishop Thomson, then in India. The ministers and laymen of the committee were gathered from every part of the Church: the East, the Center, the West, and the Pacific slope were all fairly in presence of each other in deliberation. It is believed that the Methodist Episcopal Church was thoroughly, as a whole, represented at Cleveland.

The spirit of the committee was admirable. The utmost freedom of speech prevailed; every bishop, every minister, and every layman on the committee took part in the discussions at some period of its protracted session. All opinions were compared, all interests were weighed, and all proposed plans were discussed. The great aim was so to provide for the *Connectional* interests of the Church, and for such a *Connectional* demonstration of devotion to her welfare, as not only not to interfere with local wants, but also, and to a large extent, to provide for them.

An adjourned meeting of the committee was held in New York on the 8th of November, 1865. The result of the deliberations of such a body of men, animated by such a spirit, is set forth in the final resolutions of the committee, as follows:

Resolved, That it is the sense of this committee that the Centenary Educational Fund ought to be placed before our people as the prominent object for connectional contributions.

Resolved, That if any contributors desire to specify the precise objects of their centenary subscriptions, in whole or in part, it shall be open to them to name the following objects, namely:

1. The Centenary Educational Fund.
2. The Garrett Biblical School at Evanston.
3. The Methodist General Biblical Institute at Concord, to be removed to the vicinity of Boston.
4. A Biblical Institute in the Eastern Middle States.
5. A Biblical Institute in Cincinnati or vicinity.
6. A Biblical Institute on the Pacific coast.

But contributions to these three last objects (4, 5, and 6) shall be retained and managed by the Centenary Educational Board till assured that enough has been actually raised from other sources to make the aggregate amount, including the connectional contributions to those respective objects, not less than one hundred and fifty thousand dollars in each case.

7. The erection of Centenary Missionary buildings for the Mission House at New York.
8. The Irish Connectional Fund.
9. The Biblical School at Bremen, Germany.
10. The Chartered Fund. (Such sums as contributors may desire to appropriate in that way to the support of worn-out preachers, their widows and orphans.)

Resolved, That all the unspecified funds raised throughout the Church, and also all sums specifically contributed for the "Centenary Educational Fund," be placed in the hands of a Board, to be appointed as provided in a subsequent resolution, to be called the Centenary Connectional Educational Board of the Methodist Episcopal Church.

Resolved, That the said board shall securely invest the entire principal funds, and shall appropriate the interest only from time to time, at their discretion, to the following purposes and none other, namely:

a. To aid young men preparing for the foreign missionary work of the Methodist Episcopal Church.

b. To aid young men preparing for the ministry of the Methodist Episcopal Church. These two objects to be reached through the Missionary Society, the bishops, and such educational societies of the Church as may be approved by the board.

c. To the aid of the two biblical or theological schools now in existence, and of such others as may, with the approval of the General Conference of the Methodist Episcopal Church, hereafter be established.

d. To the aid of universities, colleges, or academies now existing under the patronage of the Church, or which may hereafter be established.

Provided, 1. That no appropriation shall be made by the board at any time for building purposes, either for biblical schools, or for universities, colleges, or academies.

2. That no university, college, or academy not now in existence shall be aided by the board, unless the board shall first have been consulted, and shall have approved of the establishment and organization of such institution.

Resolved, That the board shall consist of twelve trustees, of whom two shall be bishops, four ministers, and six laymen, of which number five shall be a quorum; and no trustee shall receive any compensation for his services, except for expenses in attending the sessions of the board.

Resolved, That the board be authorized to secure a suitable charter, which shall empower the board to receive, hold, and convey real and personal estate, and to receive and administer bequests and legacies: also to fix the seat of its operations and of its place of meeting from time to time, and to appoint, if need be, a secretary and treasurer, with proper compensation, who shall be required to give suitable bonds.

Resolved, That the bishops be authorized and requested to appoint the first board, and that at its first meeting the board shall settle by lot the terms of service of its individual members in such manner that four trustees shall go out of office with each and every General Conference term of four years, and that all vacancies be filled as follows, namely: The General Conference shall nominate two persons for each vacancy, and the trustees shall choose one to fill the vacancy; provided, however, that all vacancies occurring more than six months before the session of the General Conference shall be filled by the bishops, the persons so appointed to hold office only up to the time of the General Conference, when their places shall be held as vacant, and shall be filled as aforesaid.

Resolved, That a committee be appointed, to be called "The Central Centenary Committee of Arrangements and Correspondence," whose duty it shall be to correspond with the conference Centenary Committees, to prepare and publish the necessary documents, through the periodical press and otherwise, and to make such other arrangements as may be necessary to secure the general sympathy and co-operation of the Church in the connectional part of the Centenary collections.

"*Resolved*, That a committee of six be appointed by the Chair to nominate the Central Committee."

The Chair appointed the committee of six. After a short deliberation the committee reported the following names, to constitute the "Central Centenary Committee of Arrangements and Correspondence," namely: Dr. M'Clintock, Dr. Curry, Dr. Crooks, Mr. Oliver Hoyt, Mr. James Bishop, and Mr. C. C. North.

Finally, a number of Branch Centenary Committees were appointed, and the Central Committee was authorized to appoint additional branches. A list of the committees appointed at Cleveland will be found below.

THE CENTRAL CENTENARY COMMITTEE.

The Central Committee began its sessions, in the city of New York, soon after the session of the General Committee. Its first duty was to distribute the Minutes of the General Committee, copies of which were sent to every member of that committee, to all members of the branch committees, as far as then formed, to every presiding elder throughout the Church, and to all the editors of Methodist papers.

The next step of the committee was to form additional branch committees. The General Committee had already appointed branches for the principal cities. It was thought best, in order to reach the whole Church, that a branch committee should be formed for each presiding elder's district, with the presiding elder at its head. Circulars were issued in May, 1865, to all the presiding elders, requesting them to nominate committees. In many cases the answers to this circular were long delayed, and even yet (November, 1865) some of the districts are not provided for. The Rev. W. C. Hoyt, who was appointed secretary of the committee in August, entered into a very extensive correspondence on the subject; and it is now hoped that within a few months every district in the Church will be represented. A complete list will be issued before October, 1866.

CITY BRANCH COMMITTEES.

BALTIMORE: Thomas Kelso, William Hamilton, D.D., I. P. Cook. BOSTON: N. E. Cobleigh, D.D., Hon J. Sleeper, I. Rich. BROOKLYN: Hon. M. F. Odell, John French, Samuel Truslow. BUFFALO: Rev. J. E. Robie, F. H. Root, H. H. Otis. CENTRAL NEW YORK: Rev. D. D. Lore, Mr. Wood, of Rochester, Rev. W. H. Goodwin, Samuel Luckey, D.D., G. Peck, D.D. CHICAGO: T. M. Eddy, D.D., J. V. Farwell, A. R. Scranton. CHILLICOTHE, OHIO: William T. M'Clintock, William M'Kell, O. Harmen. CINCINNATI: James F. Chalfant, Rev. J. M. Reid, D.D., Harvey De Camp. CLEVELAND, O.: H. Benton, W. P. Cook, Rev. M. Hill. CONCORD, N. H.: Rev. E. Adams, William Prescott, M.D., Hon. T. L. Tullock. COLUMBUS, O.: Rev. J. M. Trimble, D.D., J. F. Bartlett, Timothy Carpenter. DETROIT: S. Cements, Jr., D. Preston, Hon. John Owen. DENVER CITY: O. A. Willard, Gov. John Evans, Rev. B. T. Vincent. HARTFORD: Rev. M. L. Scudder, J. F. Judd, C. P. Case. INDIANAPOLIS: Rev. F. C. Holliday, D.D., O. Toucy, J. S. Dunlop. KALAMAZOO, MICH.: F. D. Hemmingly, S. W. Walker, H. Wood. MEMPHIS, TENN.: Rev. Wm. Hawkins, F. A. Marou, Dr. C. Collins. MIDDLETOWN: Rev. John Pegg, Jr., Prof. John Van Vleck, Hon. D. W. Camp. MONTPELIER, VT.: Rev. E. J. Scott, Hon. P. Dillingham, Rev. P. P. Ray. NASHVILLE, TENN.: Rev. W. H. Norris, James K. Ferris. NEWARK: C. Walsh, Rev. L. R. Dunn, Thomas Campbell. NEW HAVEN: Rev. T. H. Burch, James Punderford, W. O. Armstrong. NEW ORLEANS: Rev. J. P. Newman, D.D., Rev. W. H. Pearne, G. W. Ames. PHILADELPHIA: Joseph Castle, D.D., J. Whiteman, C. Heiskell. PITTSBURGH: Dr. S. H. Nesbit, Alexander Bradley, W. H. Kincaid. PORTLAND, ME.: E. Clark, M.D., George Webber, D.D., S. Rich. PORTLAND, OREGON: Rev. H. C. Benson, D.D., Hon. N. C. Gibbs, Rev. William Roberts. PROVIDENCE, R. I.: Hon. W. B. Lawton, Rev. Paul Townsend, J. D. Flint. SAN FRANCISCO: Rev. E. Thomas, A. Merrill, W. H. Coddington. ST. PAUL, MINN.: Rev. C. Brooks, D.D., Rev. C. Hobart, Hon. John

Nikols. St. Louis, Mo.: Rev. B. F. Crary, D.D., Gen. C. B. Fisk, S. Rich. Virginia City: Gov. H. G. Blaisdell, Rev. Thomas S. Dunn, J. Faul. Washington City: Rev. John Lanahan, D.D., Rev. B. H. Nadal, W. Woodward, Esq. Wheeling, Va.: Rev. J. Drummond, D.D., Hon. C. Hubbard, A. M. Adams. Wilmington, Del.: J. Ganse, G. W. Sparks, Rev. J. Riddle.

CENTENARY RELIGIOUS SERVICES.

The primary object of the whole Centenary celebration is declared by the General Conference to be

> The spiritual improvement of our members; and especially by reviewing the great things God hath wrought for us, the cultivating of feelings of gratitude for the blessings received through the agency of Methodism.

To carry out this object the General Conference further directs that

> Each Annual Conference shall provide for the delivery of a memorial sermon before its own body at the session next preceding the centennial celebration, and also appoint a committee of an equal number of ministers and laymen to give advice and direction for the appropriate celebration of the Centennial in our principal Churches.

The Committee, in accordance with a generally expressed desire from various parts of the Church, recommend also the following:

> That the first Sunday in January, 1866, be observed as a day of special and united prayer for the divine blessing upon the Centenary services of the year, and for a general revival of religion that the Centenary year may prove to be an epoch in the spiritual progress of the Church; and that the pastors of all our Churches be requested to read the Centenary Resolutions of the General Conference and to expound them to their people on that occasion.

That a special service be set apart in each of our societies where there is a Sunday-school, in October, 1866, for a *children's* celebration of the Centenary festival, and that suitable arrangements be made in due time by the Branch Committees in concert with the pastors and Sunday-school teachers.

That the last Sunday of October, 1866, be observed as a day of Special Centenary services, and that the Central Committee prepare and publish a proclamation and programme in reference to the observance of the day.

The Centenary Religious Services will thus include: (1.) The services of the first Sunday in January, 1866. (2.) The memorial sermon before each Annual Conference. (3.) The Church services in October, 1866, plans for which are to be suggested by the Annual Conference Committees. (4.) The Sunday-school services in October, 1866, to be arranged by the Centenary Branch Committees, in concert with pastors and Sunday-school officers. (5.) The Special Centenary Thanksgiving service of the last Sunday in October, 1866, under uniform arrangements for the whole Church.

Other religious services, such as general class-meetings, prayer-meetings, district meetings, etc., will doubtless be held, under the directions of the Presiding Elders, Pastors, and Branch Committees in the various localities.

CENTENARY CONTRIBUTIONS.

The General Conference directs (see above, p. 248) that two classes of objects, Connectional and Local, *shall* be placed before the people for their contributions. What the connectional objects shall be has been decided by the *Joint Committee of Ministers and Laymen* appointed by the General Conference for that purpose. What the local objects shall be is to be decided, in each conference, by a *Committee of Ministers and Laymen* appointed by the conference.

CONNECTIONAL OBJECTS.

The objects named for contributions by the Cleveland Committee are, as will have been seen, (pages 251 and 252,) all of a Connectional character. The first place is given to Education. The *chief* object presented to the Church, for connectional contributions, is the foundation of a Permanent Fund, to be called "The Centenary Educational Fund;" the interest only of which is to be employed in aiding our institutions of learning and in helping poor young men to prepare themselves for the ministry at home, or for the missionary work abroad. As Dr. Stevens remarks, (p. 242,) "a more practicable or more sublime design is hardly possible to the denomination." See his remarks, at the page cited, in confirmation of this broad statement. Our more thoughtful and far-seeing contributors will doubtless give to this object more largely than to any of the others named.

It is the *one* object to which every member of the Church, it is hoped, will contribute something, inasmuch as it is, of all the objects named, the most thoroughly Connectional and the most clearly monumental. A permanent fund of a million of dollars, or more, will be a monumental institution, more lasting than brass, to carry down to posterity the gratitude of the Methodists of 1866, as testified by their Centenary gifts. It will form at the same time our most beneficent legacy of the Centenary year to the century that is to follow. The rapid march of the census of American population outstrips all calculation. By the year 1900 there will be teeming millions in regions now just opened to settlement and to enterprise. Moreover, the whole South is just reopened by the extinction of the great rebellion. For all this vast population our Permanent Fund will afford a steady assistance and stimulus to effort for the great work of Christian education. Let us make this fund a grand and worthy Centenary monument. If there be failure in any part of our plan, let there be none in this.

All the other objects proposed by the Committee have, it will be seen, a Connectional character. The Committee has taken it for granted that the conferences severally will provide, in their local collections, for their colleges and academies. But the interest of *theological* education is a common and connectional one. Ministers educated at Boston or Evanston, in New York or Ohio, or even on the Pacific coast, are educated for the whole Church. They may be transferred, in a year after graduation, from the East to the West, or from the North to the South. The whole Church is interested in each of the existing theological schools, and in the new ones contemplated by the Centenary Committee, because it is the interest of the whole Church that her young men everywhere, who are called to the ministry, should have the opportunity of theological training.

The *Missionary Society* is also a thoroughly connectional interest. The society *must* have a permanent home. Its Centenary Hall will not only afford the necessary accommodation for the vast operations of the society, but will also be a permanent and visible monument of the centenary year.

The *Irish Fund* is also a connectional enterprise. There is hardly a corner of Methodism in the United States that has not been strengthened by Irish Methodism. There is not a conference which does not contain ministers from Ireland or of Irish descent. There are more Methodists from Ireland in our Church than are left in Ireland. The small contribution named by the Centenary Committee will no doubt be offered freely by the Church. Those of our members who are themselves from Ireland, or who are of Irish descent, will, no doubt, see to it that this part of our connectional plan shall not fail. And they will be aided by many others who will remember that Methodism was first planted in America by Embury and Strawbridge, both Irishmen, and who will see a special fitness in recognizing this obligation on the Centenary occasion. The very Centenary date itself is fixed by the date (1766) of the labors of Embury, the Irish local preacher, who was the honored instrument of planting Methodism in America.

The *Biblical School at Bremen* affords instruction to young men preparing for the ministry in Germany, as well as in America. Its support appeals to no single locality of Methodism, but to the whole Church. Let us remember that the Palatine Irish, among whom Embury and his associates were trained, were not Romanists, but the children of German Protestants. Let us remember, too, that our Methodist theology, and especially our Methodist view of practical and experimental religion, were originally derived by Wesley from German sources. It was the reading of Luther on Galatians that led Wesley to true faith in Christ. It was the influence of the suggestions of Böhler and the Moravians that gave his mind the first bias toward the full evangelical view of faith and its effects. (See pp. 29–32.) And with this sense of gratitude for the past, let us consult our security for the future, by doing all we can to evangelize, *in their own home*, the Germans who are to make up so large a part of the future American people.

MODES OF CONTRIBUTION.

The general modes of giving to the Centenary objects are two, contributions by individuals, and Church collections. In addition to these, special provision has been made, as will be seen below, for Sunday-school collections.

Contributions.

1. *Contributions* may be made at any time between this date and the end of October, 1866. It is suggested that, in all large cities and important towns, preliminary meetings of leading laymen be held, for information as to the plan and scope of the movement, for the distribution of Centenary documents, and for the securing of subscriptions. Liberal donations from our prominent members, at an early date, will give tone and spirit to the whole Centenary enterprise. The Pastors and Branch Committees should take pains to get up such meetings, and to see that *all contributions* be reported duly to the treasurer.

2. Contributions may be made payable in cash, or in such installments as the donor may find convenient to himself; such installments, of course, being

properly secured, to avoid trouble or litigation in case of death.

3. Donors will, in all cases, specify what amount of their contribution is intended for Connectional, and what for Local purposes. Thus, suppose that a person intends to give a certain sum, he may simply say, "I give so much to the Connectional and so much to the Local Fund." In that case his connectional sum will go to the "Permanent Educational Fund," while his local sum will be appropriated by the Conference Local Committee.

Or, he may wish to divide his connectional contributions among the several connectional objects named. In that case he may say, "I give so much to the Centenary Educational Fund; so much to the Garrett Biblical Institute, (or to the Boston Biblical Institute, etc., as the case may be;) so much for Centenary Mission Buildings at New York; so much for the Irish Fund; so much for the Biblical Institute at Bremen; and so much for the Chartered Fund." Of course, every donor may vary his relative contributions to each of these objects at his own pleasure. But let it always be borne in mind that the "Centenary Educational Fund" is the chief object to be considered.

Collections.

1. It is understood that Centenary collections will be taken, in all our churches throughout the land,

before the close of October, 1866. The collections may be fixed for some special day in that month, or may be taken up at every meeting to be held during the month, as may seem most expedient to the local authorities.

2. It is earnestly hoped that there will be universal agreement to the principle that the plate *collections*, and all unspecified contributions made in the public congregation, shall be divided equally between the Connectional and Local Funds.

3. It is suggested that as the month of October, 1866, is appropriated by the General Conference for Centenary collections, it is desirable that, as far as possible, all other special collections should be avoided in our Churches during that month.

Sunday-School Collections.

The Central Committee having called the attention of the General Committee to the importance of enlisting our Sunday-schools in the centenary movement, after fully considering the subject the following action was taken:

1. That a Sunday-school children's fund be established for the following purposes and under the following conditions: (1.) The fund to be vested in and administered by the Board of Trustees already authorized, but to be kept as a separate fund. (2.) The interest of it to be appropriated to assist meritorious Sunday-school scholars of either sex who may need help in obtaining a more advanced education. (3.) Each conference to share in the annual proceeds of this fund propor-

tionately to the number of Sunday-school children under its care. (4.) That the beneficiaries within the bounds of each annual conference be selected in such manner as each conference shall direct.

2. Each Sunday-school scholar who shall contribute one dollar to the Children's Fund, and each one who shall collect five dollars for the same, and pay that amount into the treasury, shall be entitled to receive a medal as hereinafter described.

These medals will have the head of Rev. John Wesley on one side, and that of Bishop Asbury, the pioneer Bishop of the Methodist Episcopal Church, on the other. The inscriptions will be: on one side, "Children's Medal;" and on the other, "Centenary of American Methodism, 1866."

It is recommended that a special service be set apart in each of our societies where there is a Sunday-school, in October, 1866, for a *children's* celebration of the centenary festival, and that suitable arrangements be made in due time by the branch committees, in concert with the pastors and Sunday-school officers. We think this subject as it is here presented cannot fail to secure the hearty co-operation of all our Sunday-schools—officers, teachers, scholars, and friends.

CENTENARY DOCUMENTS.

The Central Committee has commenced the publication of a series of *Centenary Documents*, which will be issued from time to time. Among these documents will be found the Resolutions of the General Conference, the Address of the Bishops, the Address of the Central Committee, Instructions to Branch Committees, and several tracts explanatory of the Centenary movement, and of its objects. These documents may be obtained of the Branch Committees, of the Book Agents at New York, Cincinnati, Chicago, and the Depositories generally, or upon application in writing to the Secretary of the Central Committee, 200 Mulberry-street, New York.

CONCLUSION.

The General Conference of 1864, after setting forth the two great channels of contribution, Connectional and Local, for the gifts of the people, appealed to the Church in the following stirring words:

As the highest authority of the Methodist Episcopal Church, we commend this whole subject to the prayerful consideration of every minister, traveling and local, and every official and private member of the Church, calling for the most systematic and energetic efforts everywhere to carry out in their true spirit these noble plans; and after due consideration, we deem it right to ask for and to expect not less than two millions of dollars for achievements which will be worthy of our great and honored Church, and which shall show to our descendants to the latest generations the gratitude we feel for the wonderful Providence which originated and has so largely blessed and prospered our beloved Church.

The sum of two millions is here named as the lowest mark at which the Church should aim in its Centenary offerings of gratitude. It is believed that this *minimum* will be largely transcended; and, indeed, that the final summing up will be nearer four millions than two. And without pretending to dictate to the ministry or the membership of the Church, we feel it our duty to make the following concluding suggestions:

1. One great object of the Centenary movement should be to promote the Connectional spirit of Methodism, and to bind anew, in cords of fraternal love and of devotion to the common cause, the East, the West, the North, and the South. So let us rebuke, by the grand unity of our vast societies, the spirit of secession, whether in Church or State. Unity in Christ is one of the needful marks of the true Church, and to promote the unity of the American people is one of the obvious functions of the Church in this country. We trust that this mark and function of the Church will be dwelt on in every pulpit of Methodism at some period of the Centenary celebration.

2. One of the most signal and obvious ways of showing our Connectional spirit will be to contribute to the Centenary Educational Permanent Fund, and to the other Connectional objects named by the General Conference and its committees. As we

have said, the whole Church, and at the same time every locality within its bounds, is interested in these objects.

Local objects will doubtless be urged, with earnestness and pertinacity, by those interested in them. We do not wish to overshadow these objects so as to hinder their success. At the same time let us remember that these objects are always with us, always at our doors, and therefore always likely to be taken care of. But our Permanent Fund is to be the great mark and proof of our connectional feeling as demonstrated by our Centenary gifts. Let the Centenary year be our Sabbath of Church fellowship; one year, at least, out of the century, in which we shall rise above all local and sectional thoughts, feelings, and interests, into the higher atmosphere of our Unity in the Church, and in Christ the Head of the Church.

CENTRAL COMMITTEE.

J. M'Clintock, D.D.,	Oliver Hoyt, Esq.,
D. Curry, D.D.,	James Bishop, Esq.,
G. R. Crooks, D.D.,	C. C. North, Esq.

W. C. Hoyt, Secretary.

General Treasurers, Carlton & Porter, 200 Mulberry-street, New York.

Local Treasurers will be appointed by each Branch Committee.

APPENDIX.

No. I.

THE GENERAL RULES.

THE NATURE, DESIGN, AND GENERAL RULES OF OUR UNITED SOCIETIES.

(1) In the latter end of the year 1739, eight or ten persons came to Mr. Wesley in London, who appeared to be deeply convinced of sin, and earnestly groaning for redemption. They desired (as did two or three more the next day) that he would spend some time with them in prayer, and advise them how to flee from the wrath to come; which they saw continually hanging over their heads. That he might have more time for this great work, he appointed a day when they might all come together; which from thenceforward they did every week, namely, on *Thursday*, in the evening. To these, and as many more as desired to join with them, (for their number increased daily,) he gave those advices from time to time which he judged most needful for them; and they always concluded their meeting with prayer suited to their several necessities.

(2) This was the rise of the United Society, first in *Europe*, and then in *America*. Such a society is no other than "*a company of men* having the form and seeking

the power of *godliness, united in order to pray together, to receive the word of exhortation, and to watch over one another in love, that they may help each other to work out their salvation.*"

(3) That it may the more easily be discerned whether they are indeed working out their own salvation, each society is divided into smaller companies, called classes, according to their respective places of abode. There are about twelve persons in a class; one of whom is styled *the leader*. It is his duty,

I. To see each person in his class once a week at least; in order,

1. To inquire how their souls prosper.

2. To advise, reprove, comfort, or exhort as occasion may require.

3. To receive what they are willing to give toward the relief of the preachers, Church, and poor.*

II. To meet the ministers and the stewards of the society once a week; in order,

1. To inform the minister of any that are sick, or of any that walk disorderly, and will not be reproved.

2. To pay the stewards what they have received of their several classes in the week preceding.

(4) There is only one condition previously required of those who desire admission into these societies, "a desire to flee from the wrath to come, and to be saved from their sins." But wherever this is really fixed in the soul, it will be shown by its fruits. It is therefore expected of all who continue therein, that they should continue to evidence their desire of salvation,

First, By doing no harm, by avoiding evil of every

* This part refers to towns and cities; where the poor are generally numerous, and Church expenses considerable.

kind, especially that which is most generally practiced; such as,

The taking of the name of God in vain.

The profaning the day of the Lord, either by doing ordinary work therein, or by buying or selling.

Drunkenness, buying or selling spirituous liquors, or drinking them, unless in cases of extreme necessity.

Slaveholding; buying or selling slaves.

Fighting, quarreling, brawling, brother *going to law* with brother; returning evil for evil; or railing for railing; the *using many words* in buying or selling.

The *buying or selling goods that have not paid the duty.*

The *giving or taking things on usury*, that is, unlawful interest.

Uncharitable or *unprofitable* conversation; particularly speaking evil of magistrates or of ministers.

Doing to others as we would not they should do unto us.

Doing what we know is not for the glory of God; as,

The *putting on of gold and costly apparel.*

The *taking such diversions* as cannot be used in the name of the Lord Jesus.

The *singing* those *songs*, or *reading* those *books*, which do not tend to the knowledge or love of God.

Softness and needless self-indulgence.

Laying up treasure upon earth.

Borrowing without a probability of paying; or taking up goods without a probability of paying for them.

(5) It is expected of all who continue in these societies, that they should continue to evidence their desire of salvation,

Secondly, By doing good; by being in every kind

merciful after their power; as they have opportunity, doing good of every possible sort, and, as far as possible, to all men.

To their bodies, of the ability which God giveth, by giving food to the hungry, by clothing the naked, by visiting or helping them that are sick or in prison.

To their souls, by instructing, reproving, or exhorting all we have any intercourse with; trampling under foot that enthusiastic doctrine, that "we are not to do good unless *our hearts be free to it.*"

By doing good, especially to them that are of the household of faith, or groaning so to be; employing them preferably to others; buying one of another; helping each other in business; and so much the more because the world will love its own, and them *only.*

By all possible *diligence* and *frugality*, that the Gospel be not blamed.

By running with patience the race which is set before them, *denying themselves, and taking up their cross daily;* submitting to bear the reproach of Christ, to be as the filth and offscouring of the world; and looking that men should say *all manner of evil of them falsely for the Lord's sake.*

(6) It is expected of all who desire to continue in these societies, that they should continue to evidence their desire of salvation,

Thirdly, By attending upon all the ordinances of God: such are,

The public worship of God:

The ministry of the word, either read or expounded:

The Supper of the Lord:

Family and private prayer:

Searching the Scriptures; and

Fasting or abstinence.

(7) These are the general rules of our societies; all which we are taught of God to observe, even in his written word, which is the only rule, and the sufficient rule, both of our faith and practice. And all these we know his Spirit writes on truly awakened hearts. If there be any among us who observe them not, who habitually break any of them, let it be known unto them who watch over that soul as they who must give an account. We will admonish him of the error of his ways. We will bear with him for a season. But if then he repent not, he hath no more place among us. We have delivered our own souls.

No. II.

ARTICLES OF RELIGION.

I. Of Faith in the Holy Trinity.

There is but one living and true God, everlasting, without body or parts, of infinite power, wisdom, and goodness; the maker and preserver of all things, visible and invisible. And in unity of this Godhead, there are three persons, of one substance, power, and eternity, the Father, the Son, and the Holy Ghost.

II. Of the Word, or Son of God, who was made very man.

The Son, who is the Word of the Father, the very and eternal God, of one substance with the Father, took man's nature in the womb of the blessed virgin; so that two whole and perfect natures, that is to say, the Godhead and manhood, were joined together in one person, never to be divided, whereof is one Christ, very God and very man, who truly suffered, was crucified, dead and buried, to reconcile his Father to us, and to be a sacrifice, not only for original guilt, but also for actual sins of men.

III. Of the Resurrection of Christ.

Christ did truly rise again from the dead, and took again his body, with all things appertaining to the perfection of man's nature, wherewith he ascended into heaven, and there sitteth until he return to judge all men at the last day.

IV. Of the Holy Ghost.

The Holy Ghost, proceeding from the Father and the Son, is of one substance, majesty, and glory with the Father and the Son, very and eternal God.

V. The Sufficiency of the Holy Scriptures for Salvation.

The Holy Scriptures contain all things necessary to salvation; so that whatsoever is not read therein, nor may be proved thereby, is not to be required of any man, that it should be believed as an article of faith, or be thought requisite or necessary to salvation. In the name of the Holy Scripture, we do understand those canonical books of the Old and New Testament, of whose authority was never any doubt in the Church.

The Names of the Canonical Books.

Genesis,
Exodus,
Leviticus,
Numbers,
Deuteronomy,
Joshua,
Judges,
Ruth,
The First Book of Samuel,
The Second Book of Samuel,
The First Book of Kings,
The Second Book of Kings,
The First Book of Chronicles,
The Second Book of Chronicles,
The Book of Ezra,
The Book of Nehemiah,
The Book of Esther,
The Book of Job,
The Psalms,
The Proverbs,
Ecclesiastes, or the Preacher,
Cantica, or Songs of Solomon,
Four Prophets the greater,
Twelve Prophets the less:

All the books of the New Testament, as they are commonly received, we do receive and account canonical.

VI. Of the Old Testament.

The Old Testament is not contrary to the New; for both in the Old and New Testament everlasting life is offered to mankind by Christ, who is the only Mediator between God and man, being both God and man. Wherefore they are not to be heard who feign that the old fathers did look only for transitory promises. Although the law given from God by Moses, as touching ceremonies and rites, doth not bind Christians, nor ought the civil precepts thereof of necessity be received in any commonwealth; yet, notwithstanding, no Christian whatsoever is free from the obedience of the commandments which are called moral.

VII. Of Original or Birth Sin.

Original sin standeth not in the following of Adam, (as the Pelagians do vainly talk,) but it is the corruption of the nature of every man, that naturally is engendered of the offspring of Adam, whereby man is very far gone from original righteousness, and of his own nature inclined to evil, and that continually.

VIII. Of Free Will.

The condition of man after the fall of Adam is such, that he cannot turn and prepare himself, by his own natural strength and works, to faith, and calling upon God; wherefore we have no power to do good works, pleasant and acceptable to God, without the grace of God by Christ preventing us, that we may have a good will, and working with us, when we have that good will.

IX. Of the Justification of Man.

We are accounted righteous before God, only for the merit of our Lord and Saviour Jesus Christ by faith, and not for our own works or deservings. Wherefore, that we are justified by faith only, is a most wholesome doctrine, and very full of comfort.

X. Of Good Works.

Although good works, which are the fruits of faith, and follow after justification, cannot put away our sins, and endure the severity of God's judgments; yet are they pleasing and acceptable to God in Christ, and spring out of a true and lively faith, insomuch that by them a lively faith may be as evidently known as a tree is discerned by its fruit.

XI. Of Works of Supererogation.

Voluntary works, besides, over, and above God's commandments, which are called works of supererogation, cannot be taught without arrogancy and impiety. For by them men do declare that they do not only render unto God as much as they are bound to do, but that they do more for his sake than of bounden duty is required: whereas Christ saith plainly, When ye have done all that is commanded you, say, We are unprofitable servants.

XII. Of Sin after Justification.

Not every sin willingly committed after justification is the sin against the Holy Ghost, and unpardonable. Wherefore, the grant of repentance is not to be denied to such as fall into sin after justification; after we have received the Holy Ghost, we may depart from grace given, and fall into sin, and, by the grace of God, rise again and amend our lives. And therefore they are to be condemned who say they can no more sin as long as they live here; or deny the place of forgiveness to such as truly repent.

XIII. Of the Church.

The visible Church of Christ is a congregation of faithful men, in which the pure word of God is preached, and the sacraments duly administered, according to Christ's ordinance, in all those things that of necessity are requisite to the same.

XIV. Of Purgatory.

The Romish doctrine concerning purgatory, pardon, worshiping, and adoration, as well of images as of relics, and also invocation of saints, is a fond thing, vainly invented, and grounded upon no warrant of Scripture, but repugnant to the word of God.

XV. Of Speaking in the Congregation in such a Tongue as the People understand.

It is a thing plainly repugnant to the word of God, and the custom of the primitive Church, to have public prayer in the Church, or to minister the sacraments, in a tongue not understood by the people.

XVI. Of the Sacraments.

Sacraments, ordained of Christ, are not only badges or tokens of Christian men's profession; but rather they are certain signs of grace, and God's good will toward us, by the which he doth work invisibly in us, and doth not only quicken, but also strengthen and confirm our faith in him.

There are two sacraments ordained of Christ our Lord in the Gospel; that is to say, Baptism and the Supper of the Lord.

Those five commonly called sacraments, that is to say, confirmation, penance, orders, matrimony, and extreme unction, are not to be counted for sacraments of the Gospel, being such as have partly grown out of the *corrupt* following of the apostles; and partly are states of life allowed in the Scriptures, but yet have not the like nature of Baptism and the Lord's Supper, because they have not any visible sign or ceremony ordained of God.

The sacraments were not ordained of Christ to be gazed upon, or to be carried about; but that we should duly use them. And in such only as worthily receive the same, they have a wholesome effect or operation; but they that receive them unworthily, purchase to themselves condemnation, as St. Paul saith. 1 Cor. xi, 29.

XVII. Of Baptism.

Baptism is not only a sign of profession, and mark of difference, whereby Christians are distinguished from others that are not baptized; but it is also a sign of regeneration, or the new birth. The baptism of young children is to be retained in the Church.

XVIII. Of the Lord's Supper.

The Supper of the Lord is not only a sign of the love that Christians ought to have among themselves one to another, but rather is a sacrament of our redemption by Christ's death; insomuch that, to such as rightly, worthily, and with faith receive the same, the bread which we break is a partaking of the body of Christ; and likewise the cup of blessing is a partaking of the blood of Christ.

Transubstantiation, or the change of the substance of bread and wine in the Supper of our Lord, cannot be proved by Holy Writ, but is repugnant to the plain words of Scripture, overthroweth the nature of a sacrament, and hath given occasion to many superstitions.

The body of Christ is given, taken, and eaten in the Supper, only after a heavenly and spiritual manner. And the means whereby the body of Christ is received and eaten in the Supper, is faith.

The sacrament of the Lord's Supper was not by Christ's ordinance reserved, carried about, lifted up, or worshiped.

XIX. Of both Kinds.

The cup of the Lord is not to be denied to the lay people; for both the parts of the Lord's Supper, by Christ's ordinance and commandment, ought to be administered to all Christians alike.

XX. Of the one Oblation of Christ, finished upon the Cross.

The offering of Christ, once made, is that perfect redemption, propitiation, and satisfaction for all the sins of the whole world, both original and actual; and there is none other satisfaction for sin but that alone. Wherefore the sacrifice of masses, in the which it is commonly said that the priest doth offer Christ for the quick and the dead, to have remission of pain or guilt, is a blasphemous fable, and dangerous deceit.

XXI. Of the Marriage of Ministers.

The ministers of Christ are not commanded by God's law either to vow the estate of single life, or to abstain from marriage: therefore it is lawful for them, as for all other Christians, to marry at their own discretion, as they shall judge the same to serve best to godliness.

XXII. Of the Rites and Ceremonies of Churches.

It is not necessary that rites and ceremonies should in all places be the same, or exactly alike; for they have been always different, and may be changed according to the diversity of countries, times, and men's manners, so that nothing be ordained against God's word. Whosoever, through his private judgment, willingly and purposely doth openly break the rites and ceremonies of the Church to which he belongs, which are not repugnant to the word of God, and are ordained and approved by common authority, ought to be rebuked openly, that others may fear to do the like, as one that offendeth against the common order of the Church, and woundeth the consciences of weak brethren.

Every particular Church may ordain, change, or abolish rites and ceremonies, so that all things may be done to edification.

XXIII. Of the Rulers of the United States of America.

The president, the congress, the general assemblies, the governors, and the councils of state, *as the delegates* *of the people,* are the rulers of the United States of America, according to the division of power made to them by the Constitution of the United States, and by the constitutions of their respective states. And the said states are a sovereign and independent nation, and ought not to be subject to any foreign jurisdiction.*

XXIV. Of Christian Men's Goods.

The riches and goods of Christians are not common, as touching the right, title, and possession of the same, as some do falsely boast. Notwithstanding, every man ought, of such things as he possesseth, liberally to give alms to the poor, according to his ability.

XXV. Of a Christian Man's Oath.

As we confess that vain and rash swearing is forbidden Christian men by our Lord Jesus Christ and James his apostle; so we judgé that the Christian religion doth not prohibit, but that a man may swear when the magistrate requireth, in a cause of faith and charity, so it be done according to the prophet's teaching, in justice, judgment, and truth.

* As far as it respects civil affairs, we believe it the duty of Christians, and especially all Christian ministers, to be subject to the supreme authority of the country where they may reside, and to use all laudable means to enjoin obedience to the powers that be; and therefore it is expected that all our preachers and people, who may be under the British or any other government, will behave themselves as peaceable and orderly subjects.

No. III.

CENSUS OF THE METHODIST EPISCOPAL CHURCH IN THE UNITED STATES.

(BY STATES.) FROM THE MINUTES OF 1864.

STATES & TERRITORIES.	Members & Probat'rs.	Preachers.*	Churches.	Value of Church Property.†	Sunday-schools.	S. S. Scholars.
Arkansas	249	1	...	....	1	60
California	4,179	77	82	$341,087	112	5,674
Colorado Territory	287	6	1	2,500	9	409
Connecticut	18,150	117	171	808,000	169	13,305
Delaware	12,289	22	119	203,225	125	8,792
District of Columbia	3,534	14	16	148,700	18	2,802
Illinois	87,961	548	896	2,147,185	1,422	83,914
Indiana	86,399	429	1,160	2,134,160	1,162	66,984
Iowa	37,599*	266	271	528,525	675	36,105
Kansas	5,462	57	34	53,640	104	3,907
Kentucky	2,677	23	38	53,320	28	1,695
Maine	22,978	170	198⅔	522,987	268	16,216
Maryland	45,987	168	514	1,128,345	415	26,805
Massachusetts	30,185	230	226	1,672,425	250	33,195
Michigan	31,434	273	260	789,450	713	34,841
Minnesota	7,681	89	70	94,275	180	6,449
Missouri	9,259	63	79	199,485	80	4,592
Nebraska	1,829	27	12	23,500	37	1,449
Nevada Territory	271	13	4	60,700	10	388
New Hampshire	10,051	87	90	268,450	110	10,225
New Jersey	45,307	237	380	1,702,625	514	43,706
New York	159,342	1,101	1,598¼	5,948,028	2,278½	155,031
Ohio	121,376	592	1,858⅓	3,273,081	1,847	125,467
Oregon	2,629	30	30	66,650	45	2,017
Pennsylvania	104,765	619	1,148	8,134,710	1,485	115,472
Rhode Island	8,225	20	20	185,200	23	8,932
Vermont	14,444	135	170⅓	385,375	208	13,766
Virginia	868	7	14	57,000	10	719
Washington Territory	278	9	4	10,100	8	890
West Virginia	15,033	74	223	201,475	174	8,829
Wisconsin	23,161	239	234	469,980	540	26,335
Total	908,889	5,743	9,922⅔	$26,614,083	13,020½	853,471

* Including those on trial and excluding superannuates. † Including parsonages.

No. IV. UNIVERSITIES AND COLLEGES.

Name.	Location.	President.	Founded.	Instructors.	Students, 1864-5. Collegiate. Classical	Students, 1864-5. Collegiate. Scientific	Students, 1864-5. All others.	Endowment.	Other Property.	Vols. in Library.
Albion College*	Albion, Michigan	G. B. Jocelyn	1860	6	10	58‡	168	......	$59,000	2,000
Alleghany College	Meadville, Pa.	George Loomis, D.D.	1815	7	51	...	91	$150,000	70,000	10,000
Baker University†	Baldwin City, Kan.	L. L. Hartman, A.M.	1858	6	24	16	164	......	100,000	500
Baldwin University*	Berea, Ohio	John Wheeler, D.D.	1856	9	16	80‡	195	33,000	28,000	1,000
Cornell College*	Mt. Vernon, Iowa	William F. King, A.M.	1857	8	15	22	386	70,000	47,000	600
Dickinson College	Carlisle, Pa.	Herman M. Johnson, D.D.	1783	7	98	84	...	70,000	75,000	24,715
Galesville University*	Galesville, Wis.	George Gale, LL.D.	1859	5	6	...	50	35,000	20,000	2,300
Genesee College*†	Lima, New York	J. W. Lindsay, D.D.	1849	5	102	...	...	92,000	53,000	3,500
German Wallace College	Berea, Ohio	William Nast, D.D.	1864	4	4	4	32	23,217	12,986	300
Hamline University*	Red Wing, Minn.	Jabez Brooks, A.M.	1854	7	25	...	310	20,000	10,000	2,000
Illinois Wesleyan University	Bloomington, Ill.	Oliver S. Munsell, D.D.	1850	6	23	30	183	25,000	30,000	1,000
Indiana Asbury University†	Greencastle, Ind.	Thomas Bowman, D.D.	1837	8	71	...	128	70,000	95,000	10,000
Iowa Wesleyan University*†	Mt. Pleasant, Iowa	Charles Elliott, D.D., LL.D.	1854	5	24	...	100	30,000	20,200	1,000
Lawrence University*†	Appleton, Wis.	George M. Steele, A.M.	1848	8	48	12	248	35,000	120,750	6,500
M'Kendree College	Lebanon, Illinois	Robert Allyn, A.M.	1834	6	35	53	139	22,000	36,500	6,500
Mount Union College*	Mount Union, Ohio	O. N. Hartshorn, LL.D.	1858	8	82	96	192	......	97,250	1,600
Northwestern University	Evanston, Illinois	Henry S. Noyes, A.M.	1855	7	39	...	94	178,565	154,373	4,000
Ohio Wesleyan University	Delaware, Ohio	Frederick Merrick, A.M.	1843	8	119	46	246	130,000	87,608	11,316
University of the Pacific*†	Santa Clara, Cal.	Edward Bannister, D.D.	1851	5	12	18	122	15,000	25,000	500
Upper Iowa University*	Fayette, Iowa	Wm. Brush, A.M.	1858	7	14	60	356	......	35,000	800
Valparaiso College†	Valparaiso, Ind.	E. H. Staley, A.M.	1859	6	49	...	264	......	23,500	400
Wesleyan University	Middletown, Conn.	Joseph Cummings, D.D.	1831	7	112	2	...	247,861	109,051	14,400
Wallamet University†	Salem, Oregon	T. M. Gatch, A.M.	1853	7	23	40	201	20,000	41,000	600
Garrett Biblical Institute	Evanston, Illinois	......	1855	3	57	...	...	110,000	.....	2,500
Methodist General Bib. Inst.	Concord, N. H.	......	1847	3	51	...	...	20,000	9,000	3,500

* Open to both sexes. † Circulars, asking for statistics, were sent to these institutions, in common with others, but no returns being received we are compelled to get the statistics from other sources, and cannot vouch for their accuracy. ‡ A four years' graduating course.

N. B.—The above table is deficient, as the columns show; Mrs. Garrett's legacy to the Garrett Biblical Institute is not included, nor the late subscriptions for the Methodist General Biblical Institute at Concord, New Hampshire.

SEMINARIES, FEMALE COLLEGES, AND ACADEMIES.

Name.	Location.	Principal.	Instructors.	Students. Male.	Students. Fem.
Amenia Seminary.........	Amenia, N. Y...	N. G. Spalding, A.M...	7	121	96
Baltimore Female College.	Baltimore, Md..	N. C. Brooks, LL.D....	12	...	120
Battle Ground Institute...	BattleGr'nd,Ind.	D. Holmes, D.D.......	6	164	130
Beaver Female Sem. & Musical Institute.....	Beaver, Pa......	R. T. Taylor, A.M.....	14	54	260
Bordentown Female Col...	Bordentown,N.J	J. H. Brakeley, A.M...	12	...	147
Brookville College	Brookville, Ind.	W. R. Goodwin, A.M..	5	50	90
Brunson Institute	Point Bluff, Wis.	G. W. Case, A.B......	5	78	107
Central Ohio Conf. Sem....	Maumee City, O.	T. M. Searles, A.B.....	3	18	22
Church Hill Institute.....	New Canaan, Ct.	J. L. Gilder, A.M......	3	20	6
Clark Seminary...........	Aurora, Illinois.	G. W. Quereau, A.M...	9	166	166
Coolville Seminary........	Coolville, Ohio..	J. P. Spahr	2	31	51
Cumberland Valley Instit.	Mechanicsb'g,Pa	Oliver Ege & Sons....	3	80	...
Dansville Seminary.......	Dansville, N. Y..	Joseph Jones, A.B.....	6	114	117
Danville Academy	Danville, Ind. ..	O. H. Smith, A.M.....	4	116	98
Danville Seminary........	Danville, Ill. ...	H. L. Dickinson, A.B..	5	80	120
Des Moines Con. Seminary.	Indianola, Iowa.	Orlando H. Baker, A.M.	4	50	75
East Genesee Conf. Sem...	Ovid, N. Y......	J. J. Brown, A.M......	6	76	90
East Maine Conf. Seminary	Bucksport, Me..	Jas. B. Crawford, A.M..	6	180	195
Eau Claire Wesleyan Sem.	Eau Claire, Wis.	S. M. White, B.A.....	3	80	56
Emory Fem. College......	Carlisle, Pa.....	R. D. Chambers, A. M.	4	...	20
Epworth Seminary........	Epworth, Iowa..	R. W. Keeler, A.M....	4	60	70
Evansville Seminary......	Evansville, Wis.	H. Colman, A.M.......	6	98	152
Falley Seminary..........	Fulton, N. Y....	J. P. Griffin, A.M......	10	239	235
Female Collegiate Institute	Santa Clara, Cal.	D. Tuthill, A.M........	9	...	67
Fort Edward Institute.....	Ft. Edward, N.Y.	Joseph E. King, D.D..	16	368	197
Ft.PlainSem.&Fem.Col.In.	Fort Plain, N.Y.	B. I. Diefendorf, A.M..	5	103	107
Fort Wayne College	Fort Wayne,Ind.	R. D. Robinson, A.M...	9	67	106
Genesee Wesleyan Sem....	Lima, New York	C. W. Bennett, A.M...	10	248	366
Gouverneur Wesleyan Sem.	Gouverneur, N.Y	George G. Dains, A.M.	6	107	178
Grand Prairie Seminary ..	Onarga, Ill......	W. Taplin, A.B........	6	149	87
Hedding Sem'y & Central Illinois Female College	Abingdon, Ill...	John T. Dickinson, A.M.	5	100	101
Hillsborough Female Col..	Hillsborough, O.	A. T. Thompson.......	10	...	210
Illinois Female College....	Jacksonville, Ill.	Charles Adams, D.D...	12	...	230
Irving Female College....	Mechanicsb'h,Pa	A. G. Marlatt, A.M....	5	...	72
Jonesville Academy.......	Jonesville, N. Y.	Fenner E. King, A.M..	6	56	4[illegible]
Maine Wesleyan Semin'y and Female College ..	Readfield, Maine	H. P. Torsey, LL.D...	9	754	845
Middlet'n In. & Prep. Sch'l.	Middletown, Ct.	Daniel H. Chase, LL.D.	8	...	89
Moore's Hill Collegiate In..	Moore's Hill,Ind.	J. A. Beswick, A.M....	6	45	55
Morgantown Fem. Col. In..	Morgantown,Va.	T. Dougherty, A.M....	6	...	80
Napa Collegiate Institute..	Napa City, Cal..	W. S. Turner, A.M....	5	45	...
Newbury Seminary and Female Collegiate In..	Newbury, Vt....	George C. Smith, A.M.	8	189	242
N. H. Conf. Sem. & Fem. Col.	Sanb'n Br., N. H.	Henry Lummis, A.M..	7	116	146
New York Conf. Sem. and Female Col. Institute.	Charlot'v'e, N.Y.	S. G. Gale, A.M........	9	90	70
Northwestern Female Col..	Evanston, Ill....	L. H. Bugbee, M.A....	7	...	100

SEMINARIES, FEMALE COLLEGES, AND ACADEMIES.—CONTINUED.

Name.	Location.	Principal.	Instructors.	Students. Male.	Students. Fem.
Ohio Wesleyan Female Col.	Delaware, Ohio.	Park S. Donelson, D.D.	10	...	306
Olney Male and Fem. Col..	Olney, Illinois..	Nelson Hawley.......	5	78	77
Oneida Conf. Seminary....	Cazenovia, N. Y.	A. S. Graves, A.M.....	9	278	257
Pennington Seminary & Female Col. Institute.	Penningt'n, N.J.	D. C. Knowles, A.M...	9	135	51
Perry Academy...........	Perry, N. Y.....	M. R. Atkins, A.M....	5	92	99
Pittsburgh Female College	Pittsburgh, Pa..	I. C. Pershing, D.D....	22	...	419
Portland Academy........	Portland, Oregon	O. S. Frambes, A.M...	5	129	115
Providence Conf. Sem. & Musical Institute.....	E.Greenw'h, R.I	J. T. Edwards, A.M...	12	164	168
Ripley Female College....	Poultney, Vt....	John Newman, D.D...	11	...	208
Rockport Collegiate Instit.	Rockport, Ind...	William S.Hooper, A.M.	5	85	90
Rock River Seminary.....	Mt. Morris, Ill..	W. T. Harlow, A.M....	6	162	128
Santiam Academy.........	Lebanon, Oregon	L. T. Woodward, A.M.	5	65	40
S. Illinois Female College..	Salem, Illinois..	M. H. Corrington, A.M.	5	...	152
Spring Mountain Acad'y..	Spring Mount., O.	J. B. Selby	1	30	39
Springfield Female College.	Springfield, Ohio.	J. H. Herron, A.M.....	6	...	114
Springfield Wes. Sem'ary and Female Col. Instit.	Springfield, Vt..	A. M. Wheeler, A.M...	10	105	271
Springville Academy.	Springville, N.Y.	David Copeland, A.M..	6	100	118
Stockton Female Institute.	Stockton, Cal...	H. W. Hunt, A.M.....	5	21	58
Stockwell Colleg. Institute	Stockwell, Ind..	H. G. Jackson, A.B....	4	77	92
Thorntown Academy......	Thorntown, Ind.	O. H. Smith, A.M.....	5	124	157
Umpqua Academy........	Wilbur, Oregon.	T. F. Royal...........	4	60	50
Waterloo Academy	Waterloo, Wis..	A. M. Stephens	4	48	67
Wesley Academy	Wesley, Ind.....	J. H. and A. Orear....	3	97	59
Wesleyan Academy.......	Wilbraham, Mass	Edward Cooke, D.D...	10	286	232
Wesleyan Female College.	Cincinnati, Ohio	Richard S. Rust, D.D..	15	...	131
Wesleyan Female College..	Wilmington, Del.	John Wilson, A.M.....	11	...	165
Western Reserve Seminary	W.Farmingt'n, O	J. M. Leonard, A.M...	8	120	156
West River Classical Instit.	West River, Md.	R. G. Chaney, A.M....	3	75	...
Whitewater College..	Centerville, Ind.	W. H. Barnes, A.M....	6	...	204
Williamsp't Dickinson Sem.	Williamsport, Pa.	T. Mitchell, D.D.......	10	311	...
Willoughby Collegiate Inst.	Willoughby, O..	J. B. Robinson, A.M...	9	73	181
Wyoming Seminary.......	Kingston, Pa....	Reuben Nelson, D.D..	15	290	260
Xenia Female College.....	Xenia, Ohio.....	William Smith, A. M..	9	37	192

SUMMARY.—TWENTY-THREE Colleges, TWO Biblical Institutes, and SEVENTY-SEVEN Seminaries, Female Colleges, and Academies. These tables are very deficient.

THE END.